Bobbing Head Dolls
1960-2000

Tim Hunter

© 1999 by
Tim Hunter

Published by

krause publications

700 E. State Street • Iola, WI 54990-0001
Telephone: 715/445-2214

Please, call or write us for our free catalog of antiques and collectibles publications. To place an
order or receive our free catalog, call 800-258-0929. For editorial comment and further information,
use our regular business telephone at (715) 445-2214

Library of Congress Catalog Number: 9967144
ISBN: 0-87341-802-6

Printed in the United States of America

Readers can contact the author, Tim Hunter, at 4301 W. Hidden Valley Dr., Reno, NV 89502;
(775) 856-4357, or email at: *tlhunter@webtv.net*

19.95

Table of Contents

Japanese-Made Dolls: 1960-1972

Introduction

Baseball

Football

Hockey

Basketball

Non-Sports

Post-Japan

Bobbing Head Team Checklist (Japan made)

Introduction

When you see a bobbing head doll, it doesn't take long to figure out why they're so popular among collectors. Beautiful colors, themes of sports teams and popular characters, plus the cool bobbing or nodding heads, combine to make these dolls hot collectibles.

The heyday of vintage bobbing head dolls was from the early-1960s to the early-1970s. It was about 15 years ago that bobbing head collecting really took off. Kids of the 1960s decided to recapture their childhoods and began collecting bobbing heads. It didn't take long before prices skyrocketed. There wasn't a huge supply of collectible dolls available. Many of the original dolls had been damaged or destroyed. Because the dolls were made from fragile *papier mâché*, cracks, chips and other misfortunes were common.

With the price of an item being set by supply and demand, prices soared as more and more collectors entered the hobby. There appears to be no slowing down for these items for year 2000 and beyond.

I've been involved in buying and selling bobbing head dolls for 18 years. This price and identification guide is a culmination of my years of handling thousands of different dolls. I also hope this guide will "set the record straight," in as much as helping to educate bobbing head buyers and sellers. Over the years, I've seen many inexperienced collectors get taken by dishonest sellers. I've seen inexperienced sellers often overprice the dolls they find. With this guide, I believe we can all become better educated buyers and sellers, making this hobby even greater than it is today.

Using the Guide

Over the years, I often got calls concerning a "Senators" doll, for example, that somebody had. What was

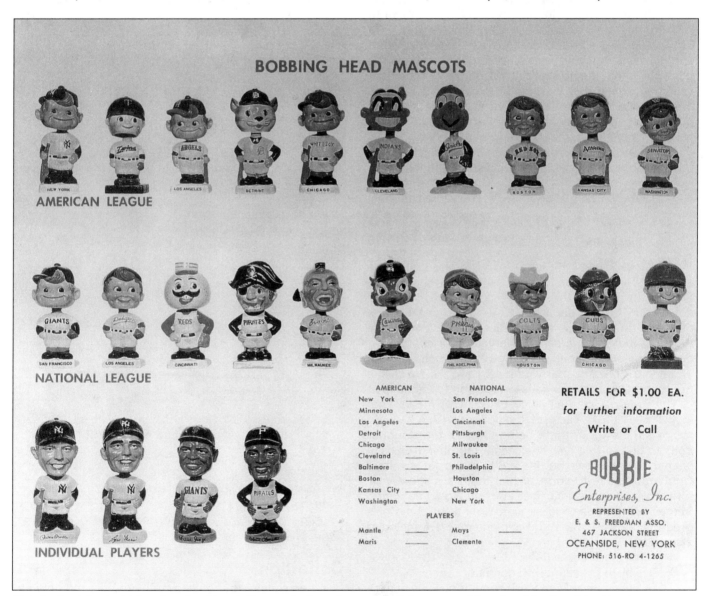

Original ad for bobbing heads. At a dollar each, it makes you wish you could go back in time! (author)

it worth? Before I could answer that question properly, I needed to know a whole lot more about the doll than just "Senators." As far as I know, there are 16 different dolls issued representing that franchise. I needed to narrow it down some!

The first thing I needed to understand was which set it belonged to. To find out about your doll, you'll need to do the same. Let's say you have a Cleveland Browns doll (an NFL franchise at that time). You've bought this guide, and now you are ready to go. Notice first, the base shape and color. These two elements will narrow your search considerably. Most all of the chapter headings contain information on one of the terms or the other. Your Browns doll has a round gold base. Of the 15 chapters or sets, three mention round gold bases. We can look at those three chapters first.

Now let's look at the doll's features. Examine the head, face and body design. You'll see terms such as "Realistic Face," "Toes-Up" and "Ear Pads" describing certain football sets. Gather the information and turn to the relevant chapters. Here it would be Chapters 16-18, in which the photos will confirm whether you need to look further. You discover, in Chapter 17, that your Browns doll has a "man" or "Realistic" face, instead of the more typical "boy" face. Lucky you! You see in the price guide that the doll sells for $450 in mint condition. You may notice that another Browns gold base doll, this one with the "boy face," is worth considerably less ($150). Recognize the difference, and this book has paid for itself a few times over.

Now that you have found the doll, you can check the pricing table. The franchises are listed alphabetically. Next is the RI or "rarity index." A number of readers may choose to skip this and head to the value columns.

Team	RI	EX	NM	M
Cleveland Browns	7/8	$150	$325	$450

Rarity Index. The rarity index number is a collector's number. This number let's you know the chances of finding the doll in the general population of sports dolls. From 1 (most common) to 10 (ultra rare) it points out true rarity within the set and sports dolls as a whole. It may give tips on undervalued or overvalued dolls. (Non-sports dolls will be given no such number. There are way too many non-sports dolls to give a number that makes any sense in relation to the price.)

The Browns doll has an RI of 7/8. This means that <u>inside</u> the Realistic Face set, the doll was a 7. A 7 would roughly translate to there being three of four tougher dolls to find in that set. The second number, ironically is an 8. How can this be HIGHER than the set number? One would have to surmise that there are some very rare dolls in the Realistic Face set. You would be right!

Values. The three figures correspond to the doll's grade. Grading photos and explanations are included elsewhere.

For the Browns dolls:
$150: Doll in Excellent (EX) condition.
$325: Doll in Near Mint (NM) condition.
$450: Doll in Mint (M) condition.

These are retail prices. These are prices that the collector should figure on paying. As in all guides, it is an estimate. If selling to a dealer you should get at least 60% to 70% of the guide value.

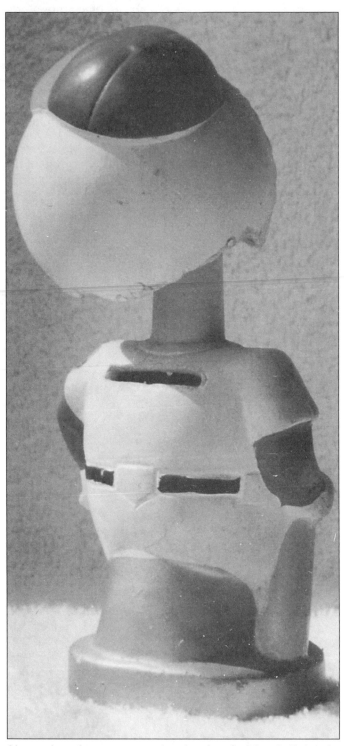

Note the damage on the back of this doll bank. Damage like this is an all-too-common occurrence. (Jack McGuire)

Condition

When selling your dolls it will always come down to condition. Let's look at the grades used in this guide.

6

Excellent (EX) condition: A doll with average wear. Any doll with a number (I use 3-4 as a cutoff) of small flaws such as thin hairline cracks, micro paint chips etc. Or a pleasing doll that has one or two large flaws such as large paint chip or larger crack. No missing pieces! Any doll that is missing a piece or has been repaired can only hope to get about 10% of mint price.

Near Mint (NM) condition: One or two small flaws. Most dolls fall in this category.

Mint (M) condition: No flaws whatsoever. No cracks, hairlines, paint chips, etc.

A doll that is "mint in box" or exhibits the same qualities, especially color and gloss, is often graded "gem mint." One can expect a decent premium over "mint" for this sort of doll.

Finally you must look at the decals. Especially those on base or chest. Decals can be flawed in many ways. From being gone altogether, put on wrong at factory or, most common, chipped or cut away. Major decal flaws can be fatal even in a doll that is mint in the box. With decal problems, you would need to subtract 30% to 60% of the doll's value to find its correct value.

Descriptions Used

Descriptions of the dolls are broken into the following areas:

Timeline: This is a general guess on what years the dolls "circulated." You will find that many of the sets have year designations. This is more shorthand than actual fact.

How to Tell: Identifying features that make this set unique or define the set further.

Set Profile: This is meant give you an overview of the set as a whole. What makes the set special, different, highlights in the set, oddities, etc.

Typical Flaws: Where to look for trouble or repairs. What to take into consideration when measuring grade.

Historical Notes: Bobbing heads were often a reflection of the times. We go back to those times in this section.

Stumbling Block: The toughest doll to acquire in any given set.

Need an Example? The other end of the spectrum.

Repairs: What to Look For

In every dream house, a heartache.

And so it seems with bobbing heads, as far as repaired dolls go. The repair artists and dealers who knowingly sell them will tell you there's nothing wrong with "restoring" a doll. It is done all the time with cars and furniture, they say. Fair enough, but given the choice of owning a repaired doll or an original gem mint doll, the collector will choose the original one ALL the time. Many collectors (including myself) would never tolerate owning a repaired doll and putting it on the

shelf next to the genuine article. It would contaminate the scene. This is how the crooked dealer makes his money. Despite the fact that he's selling a repaired doll, he's charging the same price as an original gem mint!

Let's say there's a very rare doll with a large piece of the back of the head missing at a local antique mall. In mint condition, the book says this doll is worth $1,500. The dealer is being reasonable—he marks it at 10% of book value ($150) due to the heavy damage. It ends up in the hands of a repair artist who, in very short time (as *papier mâché* is a very easy medium to work with), has repaired the damage. Time taken: 2-3 hours. Materials: 5 cents of paper, glue and paint.

What do you think he'll ask for it now!!!! You're right: $1,500! A quick $1,350 paper profit!

Of course, the collector gets stuck holding the bag. He may go for years without knowing that the doll has been repaired. Only when he goes to sell it will the terrible folly of his purchase be made known. As a dealer in the dolls, it has been my unpleasant experience many times to break the bad news to collectors selling their collection. Particularly sad are the collectors who had the foresight to buy bobbing heads in the 1980s and early-1990s. Not only do they lose most of the original price they paid, but years of exponential price increases. When a repaired doll is made known, it's price generally fetches 10% of book—just as if it had a large piece missing in the back of the head.

The cost/knowledge curve in learning to spot repairs can be ugly. The best way to avoid getting burned is to not deal with known repair artists. (they are well known by collectors in the core hobby). However, more people are entering the hobby every day and many are joining the club of bobbing head suckers. To try and stay out of this group, pay attention to the following:

- Check the rear of the doll first. This is the spot that most dolls are prone to damage. Does the paint in the rear (or anywhere else) match up with the paint on the rest of the doll?
- Look inside the head. Do you see any evidence of caulking? If you did see a funny area of paint, you'll almost certainly see a corresponding caulking area inside the head. While you're looking there, look for visible cracks. A large crack on the outside could be painted over. It will still show up on the inside.
- Many collectors told me that black light works to highlight recent additions.
- Check the doll's neck and ankles. Many dolls were cleanly snapped there and reglued. Again, look at the paint carefully around these areas.
- For the collector who knows his way around a bit, but is still unsure about a doll or two, here's a hint: Shake the head of a doll you know is a good one. Listen to the sound it makes. Shake the repaired doll's head and the sound you get is noticeably "sharper."
- Sometimes you can get a clue by looking at the bottom of the base at the stamp or sticker (turn

the doll upside down). True mint/gem mint dolls will almost always have crisp, clean stamps or stickers. If the doll looks like new but the sticker or stamp doesn't, chances are it has been fixed (repaired) for a quick sale.

- Repaints are also somewhat predictable when you have a doll with high points or sharp edges. The tip of the bonnet feather on the Cleveland Indians doll, for example. The feather tips on the St. Louis Cardinals bird head. Any doll with *mucho* detail. It is no surprise that the Warner Brothers dolls from the 1960s are repaired with abandon.
- Some dolls have fake decals. A generic elephant ($25) becomes "Dumbo" ($250) through the magic of $1 worth of hobby shop decals. (By the way there is no true "Dumbo the Elephant" doll.) Fortunately, these are easy to spot. Even for an amateur. If the decal peels at all, even the tiniest bit, it's fake. Japanese decals can only be chipped away.

Collectors are the usually some of the nicest and most harmless people in the world. All they want to do is add to their collections. That is why it is so sad that there are so many dealers in all areas of collecting, not just bobbing head dolls, that are all too willing to take advantage of their eagerness to add to their collections. Collectors deserve much better.

About the Author

Tim Hunter is one of the world's leading authorities in vintage bobbing head dolls. He has bought and sold these dolls for nearly 20 years. Readers can contact Hunter at 4301 W. Hidden Valley Dr., Reno, NV 89502; (775) 856-4357, or email at: *tlhunter@webtv.net*.

Tips on Collecting Bobbing Head Dolls: A Collector's View

(The following article was written by collector Bruce Stjernstrom)

I never owned a bobbing head doll until 1988. But like many Baby Boomers, I remember seeing them at my hometown ballpark. For me, that was Metropolitan Stadium in Bloomington, Minnesota, at a Twins game in the early-1960s. My dad would give me a couple of dollars to buy hot dogs and souvenirs. I would stand in front of the souvenir stand for what seemed like hours, looking at the displays of buttons, pennants, player photos, mini bats, pens, hats and so on. I remember thinking that the bobbing heads were pretty neat, but too expensive for me at $1.50, especially when I had to buy food, too. I usually bought the yearbook for 50 cents.

When I finally bought that first bobbing head in 1988, I was already an avid sports card collector. I had seen a few dolls at shows and decided to buy one. My first purchase was, predictably, a blue base Minnesota Twins doll I'd seen as a boy. Over the next few months, I bought a few more Twins and Vikings dolls. Before long, I bought some white base baseball, then green base and gold base, football, hockey and more. Today, my collection includes more than 700 pieces and continues to grow.

Collecting bobbing heads is not a big hobby like sports card collecting. Part of the reason for the shortage of collectors is the difficulty in finding dolls in nice collectible condition. Bobbing heads weren't popular in the 1960s and 1970s, and few survived in collectible condition. As a result, top-condition dolls are truly valuable.

Tim Hunter asked me to pass on a few tips about collecting, based on my experience. I was honored to be asked. Here are some of tips and pieces of advice about collecting bobbing heads that might be of value:

1. Decide what to collect. It could be a team (Twins) or a series (gold base baseball or college football). It doesn't matter what you decide to collect, but it helps to have goals. The important point is to collect for enjoyment's sake. That how I've kept interested in this hobby for more than 12 years.

2. Finding dolls. Finding bobbing head dolls takes a bit of time to figure out. You may have some success finding them at memorabilia shows, antique stores and sports card shops. Areas in which sports teams have been established for a long time (New York, Philadelphia, Boston, Pittsburgh) are your best bets. However, I never had much luck finding bobbing heads this way. For me, the best way to find dolls is to scour the ads in collectible magazines such as **Toy Shop** and **Sports Collectors Digest**. Once you learn who you can reliably buy from, you're on track to meet more collectors and dealers to buy, sell and trade with.

3. Quality. Decide on the level of quality you want to collect. If you're concerned about investment value, only buy dolls in near mint or better condition. Quality collectibles provide the highest return and are easier to sell, if that time ever comes. If you're collecting top quality dolls, be very patient and wait for top quality items. If you aren't as concerned about quality and are looking for some nice display pieces, you can choose "excellent" graded dolls and save 50% to 75% and have a lot more to choose from. If you're unsure and money is not a concern, buy the best, and you can't go wrong.

4. Displaying and taking care of your collection. It's best to display dolls in enclosed cases, preferably glass cases. This will keep dust and grime from making their way onto the finish. Keep the dolls out of direct sunlight, away from heat or cold and out of smoky rooms. The paint and decals are fragile, so it is not a good idea to use strong cleaners or to dust them often. Handle the dolls with care as the *papier mâché* construction is fragile and can be easily cracked. It is a good idea to keep a tissue "collar" around the neck to prevent the head from hitting the shoulders. Also make sure you have insurance that covers your collection in case of theft or fire.

5. A word of warning. While collecting bobbing heads is a lot of fun, recent high prices have brought a few seedy dealers and collectors to the hobby. Be aware that dolls are being repaired and repainted and sold as original mint dolls. Some of the paint and repair work is very obvious, but some are so good that only experienced collectors and dealers can detect it. There's nothing wrong with buying a repaired and repainted doll, as long as it's sold as such. Investment collectors consider repaired and repainted dolls to be nearly worthless.

6. Never stop learning. Learn as much about the hobby as you can. Knowledge is power. When I started collecting, I called dealers and collectors and talked for hours about bobbing heads, making notes and updating lists regularly. They might have considered me a pest in the beginning, but I've met some great people who I still enjoy discussing bobbing heads with. I learn more every week, and I think I've helped a few people myself along the way. As you learn, you will be able to quickly identify a bobbing head you come across at a flea market. You should be able to check it for flaws and assign a condition and approximate value. You should know if it's in original condition or if it's been repaired and repainted. To enjoy the hobby, it's important to know what you're buying. If you consistently overpay for poor quality merchandise, you will likely lose interest in collecting.

This book was written to enhance your collecting knowledge and enjoyment. Read it and learn as much as you can. You'll be glad you did. Happy hunting!

Some of the first dolls Stjernstrom bought were Minnesota Vikings.

Baseball Bobbing Heads

For baseball dolls, assume, *unless mentioned otherwise*, the following:

1. Sets have all representative teams from the appropriate time period.
2. Dolls are 6 inches to 7 inches tall.
3. There is no price difference for such factors as holding a bat or ball or hair style or color.
4. Baseball mascot heads: Detroit Tigers have a tiger head; Cleveland Indians have Chief Wahoo; St. Louis Cardinals and Baltimore Orioles have bird heads; Chicago Cubs have a bear head; Cincinnati Reds have Mr. Red or Ball Head; the Pittsburgh Pirates have a pirate head; and the Milwaukee/Atlanta Braves have an Indian brave head.
5. A doll in its original generic box is worth a 5% to 10% premium. For custom illustrated boxes, add 20% to 25%.
6. Cardinals and Orioles are always on diamond-shaped bases.
7. Decals will have city on base and nickname on chest.
8. A "Made in Japan" stamp or sticker will be on the bottom of base.

New York Yankees doll. An identical 15-inch promo is known. (author)

The first New York Mets doll. (Jack McGuire)

Chapter 1

1960-61 Square Color Base

BASEBALL

Timeline: Most likely the very first baseball set. Probably issued in 1960-61.

How to Tell: All dolls are on a square base of various colors except Orioles which is on a green diamond shaped base. They stand 6-inches tall. No city designation on base.

Set Profile: Unusual in a number of ways. No mascot heads besides the Orioles and Pirates. Cubs and Reds are "boy heads" in this set. All boy heads identical. No variations in hat or hair style. Not all teams were included in set. Teams are on different colored bases (base colors listed with price guide). One of two baseball sets to include major and Minor League teams (three PCL franchises here).

Typical Flaws: All heads connected to neck by older model "hook spring." This can result in dolls head sagging or displaying at a poor angle. Unfortunately nothing much can be done to solve this, as this type of spring is impossible to work with. Dolls in this set tend to be faded. Gem mint examples (exception of ultra common Twins and Angels) are quite difficult to find.

Significant Variations: A 15-inch promo New York Yankee doll is known..

Historical Notes: Contains only example of the "original" Washington Senators...Two expansion teams Mets and Los Angeles Angels introduced...Only example of Seattle (the Raniers) as a minor league city...Interesting that the non-existent Senators doll was pictured for years in advertising for Manny's Baseball Land.

Stumbling Block: The Senators doll of this set is one of the rarest dolls in the hobby. I imagine its production run was severely curtailed due to their impending relocation to Minnesota. Have seen only three or four examples of this in 20 years.

Want an example? Twins one of most common dolls in hobby.

PCL Tacoma Giants. (Jack McGuire)

PCL Portland Beavers doll. (Jack McGuire)

1960-1961 Square Color Base

Team	Base Color	RI	EX	NM	M
Baltimore Orioles	Green (diamond)	6/5	$110	$150	$190
Boston Red Sox	Green	7/6	$100	$200	$400
Chicago Cubs	Blue	5/5	$90	$140	$250
Cincinnati Reds	Red	7/6	$130	$200	$450
Los Angeles Angels	Dark Blue	2/2	$40	$60	$90
Minnesota Twins	Dark Blue	1/1	$40	$60	$90
New York Mets	Blue	7/6	$100	$175	$290
New York Yankees	Orange	4/3	$80	$120	$160
Pittsburgh Pirates	Gold	4/4	$100	$140	$180
San Francisco Giants	Orange	4/4	$80	$120	$150
Washington Senators	Dark Blue	10/10	$450	$750	$1,400

Pacific Coast League Teams

Team	Base Color	RI	EX	NM	M
Portland	Dark Blue	6/5	$100	$130	$190
Seattle	Red	8/8	$150	$250	$350
Tacoma	Orange	5/5	$100	$150	$225

Others of genre: Wood Base

Team	Base Color	RI	EX	NM	M
Los Angeles Angels	Orange	9/8	$200	$275	$375
San Francisco Giants	Orange	9/8	$250	$350	$450

Wood base Giants. (Jack McGuire)

Wood base Dodgers. (Jack McGuire)

No decal on hat and base are standard on this Baltimore Orioles doll. (Jack McGuire)

The Pittsburgh Pirates is one of only two mascot heads in first set. (Jack McGuire)

Ultra rare Washington Senators doll. The value on this doll is decreased by 20% to 25% due to the head and spring being twisted. (Jack McGuire)

Chapter 2

1961-1962 White Base Miniatures

Timeline: Almost certainly issued 1961-1962.

How to Tell: Dolls stand 4-1/2-inches tall. All on round white bases, most still having magnets in the bottom.

Set Profile: Only miniature set, besides hockey, ever produced. Quite a few different face and hair styles included in this set. Most likely a companion set to regular size white base dolls, although it probably came first. Therefore, the debut of the mascot heads for the Tigers, Indians, Braves, Reds, Cubs and Cardinals. Contains Mantle and Maris dolls. No Clemente or Mays examples. Astros doll mentioned in guide came later and may or may not be an actual part of the set. Sold, in some cases, in boxed set of 10 (AL & NL). Mantle and Maris dolls came in custom boxes. Add 50% to Mantle price for box and 10% on Maris.

Typical Flaws: Very thin neck. Many times, the neck snapped cleanly and was re-glued. Look very carefully at end of neck when purchasing miniatures. If doll is repaired, it would most likely be there.

Significant Variations: Minneapolis Twins example is an interesting historical note. Would guess 15% of Twins dolls have the city's (instead of the state) name on base. Maris and Mantle minis come with either a script "NY" or "Yankees." No premium yet established either way. Tigers and Indians also come on round green bases. White base examples are rarer. Los Angeles Angels doll can very rarely be found with an "Anaheim" paper sticker on base. Much more common is the regular size example. Mets doll can be found with blue shoes about 20% of the time. Orioles doll also comes with an extremely rare boy head. Probably a one day "error run."

Historical Notes: Los Angeles Angels trip to Orange County, immortalized with "Anaheim" doll. Also foretold future it seems...Debut of expansion dolls from Houston and Washington...Only Pirates doll to hold a bat.

Stumbling Block: The Mickey Mantle miniature has, despite his prominence in the hobby, always been very difficult to find, especially in nice shape. Minneapolis doll probably second. Cardinal doll tricky due to a lot of snapped necks.

Want an example? Dodgers and Angels must have flooded local market. The Yankees are gaining ground due to large finds in the past few years.

Miniature Pirates dolls. Note: Doll on left has a fake decal on base. On white base Pirates dolls, Pittsburgh is always separated between the "S" and "B." (Jack McGuire)

Regular Roger Maris at left and mini Maris. (Jack McGuire)

1961-1962 White Base Miniatures (all round white base)

Team	RI	EX	NM	M
Anaheim Angels	10/10	$200	$350	$500
Baltimore Orioles	5/6	$225	$340	$500
Boston Red Sox	6/6	$200	$300	$475
Chicago Cubs	6/6	$250	$400	$700
Chicago White Sox	5/5	$120	$150	$275
Cincinnati Reds	6/6	$150	$300	$500
** Cleveland Indians	6/6	$250	$350	$600
** Detroit Tigers	6/6	$250	$325	$550
Houston Colt .45s	6/6	$150	$225	$350
Houston Astros	7/7	$125	$240	$425
Los Angeles Angels	1/2	$75	$100	$150
Los Angeles Dodgers	1/2	$75	$100	$140
Kansas City A's	6/6	$140	$225	$325
Milwaukee Braves	7/7	$200	$350	$700
Minnesota Twins	6/6	$140	$200	$335
Minneapolis Twins	8/8	$250	$400	$650
New York Mets	7/7	$250	$350	$550
New York Yankees	3/3	$100	$150	$250
Philadelphia Phillies	5/5	$100	$150	$240
Pittsburgh Pirates	6/7	$200	$400	$600
St. Louis Cardinals	7/8	$275	$450	$900
San Francisco Giants	5/5	$135	$180	$250
Washington Senators	6/6	$140	$250	$375

The Baltimore Orioles also has "boy head" variation that's very rare and valued at $600-$900.

**Cleveland and Detroit dolls on green bases are valued at 20% less than stated prices.*

Player	RI	EX	NM	M
Mickey Mantle	9/9	$750	$1,400	$1,950
Roger Maris	5/4	$325	$400	$500

Miniature Reds dolls. Note that each mini came with a bat or a ball. (Jack McGuire)

Mantle and Maris minis with custom boxes. These dolls had only a bat. (Jack McGuire)

Various miniature dolls. Note the variety of face and hair styles. (Jack McGuire)

This New York Mets mini is sometimes found with blue shoes. This face style is known as the "Moon Face." (Jack McGuire)

Colt .45s miniature doll. (Jack McGuire)

Mini Boston Red Sox doll. (Jack McGuire)

Regular Mickey Mantle at right and mini Mantle. (Jack McGuire)

Houston Astros team-issue miniature and regular size dolls. (Jack McGuire)

Milwaukee Braves mini doll. (Jack McGuire)

The Cleveland Indians mini comes on a green or a white base. (Jack McGuire)

Chapter 3

1961-1963 White Base

Timeline: Between the years 1961-1963.

How to Tell: Dolls on square white base.

Set Profile: The first complete set in the standard 6-1/2-inch size. All mascot heads included. Houston Colt .45s, making its doll debut, has a cowboy hat. Set included Mantle, Maris and two new additions from the NL—Willie Mays and Roberto Clemente. Custom boxes for Mantle and Maris worth 15% to 20% premium. First run of dolls had a custom box (picture of actual doll on label). All except Angels and Colts extremely rare.

Typical Flaws: Dolls, especially those done in red and blue, tend to have color fade. Hat brims are susceptible to chipping (check there for repaints). Cardinals head was too large for spring and always hangs down. Doll also has number of pointed feathers in rear which are nearly always chipped (check there for repaints). Significant premium noted for Cardinals doll in *true mint.* Early dolls had hook spring. Same problems as detailed Chapter 1.

Significant Variations: Colt .45s doll had about 5% of its run done with an all blue jersey and pants. (Beware of repaints). "Anaheim" doll mentioned in miniature section. Giants and Dodgers dolls have about 5% of the run done with decals on the chest instead of embossed lettering. Yankees doll comes with or without grooved pinstripes.

Historical Notes: One "Minneapolis Twins" regular size doll has been found... A prototype no doubt, as it found with a Twins front office exec... A photo of this doll was also used in a 1963 *Sporting News* advertisement selling dolls.

Stumbling Block: Without the Colt variation, this is not an extremely hard set to complete. Clemente has been a stumbling block historically, tough, but there are still 200-300 of those out there. Reds and Pirates are toughest of regular issues.

Want an Example? Like the miniatures, the Dodgers and Angels lead the way.

Collage of white base baseball dolls. (author)

1961-1963 White Base (all on square white bases)

Team	RI	EX	NM	M
Anaheim Angels	5/6	$80	$130	$150
Baltimore Orioles	6/6	$150	$275	$450
Boston Red Sox	5/5	$90	$130	$190
Chicago Cubs	5/6	$240	$325	$450
Chicago White Sox	7/6	$140	$180	$280
Cincinnati Reds	8/7	$200	$350	$500
Cleveland Indians	6/6	$250	$400	$700
Detroit Tigers	5/6	$150	$240	$375
Houston Colt .45s	4/4	$125	$175	$275
Houston Colt .45s (blue uniform)	9/9	$300	$500	$800
Los Angeles Angels	2/3	$75	$110	$150
*Los Angeles Dodgers	1/3	$60	$90	$125
Kansas City A's	6/6	$140	$190	$250
Milwaukee Braves	5/5	$150	$250	$400
Minnesota Twins	7/7	$130	$200	$375
New York Mets	7/7	$175	$280	$400
New York Yankees	5/5	$120	$175	$260
Philadelphia Phillies	4/5	$75	$100	$140
Pittsburgh Pirates	9/8	$250	$375	$600
St. Louis Cardinals	6/6	$175	$250	$800
*San Francisco Giants	6/6	$135	$190	$325
Washington Senators	5/6	$140	$220	$330

Los Angeles Dodgers and San Francisco Giants both have decal (usually embossed) on chest variation, which adds a 40% to 50% premium to the stated values.

First-run blue uniform Colt .45s doll. (Jack McGuire)

Regular issue white uniform Colt .45s. It comes with or without "crossed pistols" decal on hat and base. (Jack McGuire)

Player	RI	EX	NM	M
*Roberto Clemente	9/9	$750	$1,100	$1,850
**Mickey Mantle	5/5	$300	$500	$800
Roger Maris	5/5	$300	$375	$500
*** Willie Mays, dark face	5/6	$275	$400	$500
*** Willie Mays, light face	5/6	$175	$260	$400
Willie Mays, gold base	10/10	$400	$700	$1,500

Despite what most think, Clemente did come with a box. It was generic, but stamped on side "Ruberto Clemente."
*** Mantle also comes on round white base. No premium added.*
**** The light face Mays doll has a sticker on the bottom of the base and the dark face Mays doll has a stamp on the bottom of the base.*

Rarer "decal variation" white base Giants. (Jack McGuire)

Regular embossed white base San Francisco Giants. (Jack McGuire)

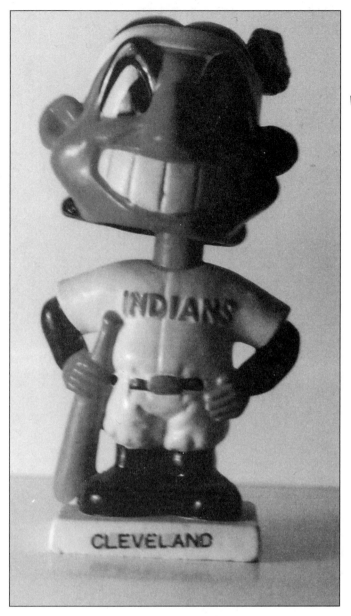

White base Cleveland Indians. (Jack McGuire)

This Pittsburgh Pirates doll is the key to white base series. Note that the two-word base decal is correct. (Jack McGuire)

Dodger white base decal (left) and embossed (right) comparison. (Jack McGuire)

If the head is off the spring, as is the case with this Cubs dolls, use simple plumbing caulk to reattach. (author)

A tough doll to find in **mint** condition is this New York Yankees white base. (Jack McGuire)

Anaheim Angels white base doll. If you peeled the paper on base, you would find a "Los Angeles" decal. (Jack McGuire)

Light face Willie Mays doll at left; dark face Mays at right. (Jack McGuire)

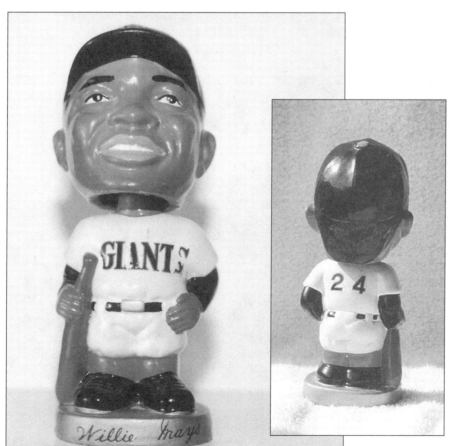

Back of gold base Willie Mays. (Jack McGuire)

Very rare gold base Willie Mays. Note the legible signature. (Jack McGuire)

Square base Roger Maris. (Jack McGuire)

Roberto Clemente doll. The "S" or the "P" on chest is often chipped. (Jack McGuire)

Round and square base Mickey Mantle comparison. Note the body mold difference. There is also an example known with a square base body on a round base. (Jack McGuire)

Chapter 4

1963-1965 Black Players

Timeline: Most likely issued in 1963-1965.

How to Tell: African-American players on round green base. Bottom of base stamped "1962."

Set Profile: This is what could be described as an experimental set. Numbers produced were very small and I doubt very much if they were a sales winner.

Two different face types in this set:

Type 1: Regular face. Not too much different than a white player painted brown. No eyebrows.

Type 2: Realistic face. Doll much more African-American in design. Larger lips and noses. This doll has eyebrows.

I believe that Type 1 is the rarer overall doll (Orioles dolls are a huge exception.) However, both versions are rare enough that no real price premium has developed either way. Realistic faces are more in demand, however, and that could change. The jury is still out on if both examples were produced for all teams. Both sides have good arguments for which face came first.

Typical Flaws: This was an extremely solid mold. The Type 2 example is especially solid, thicker in construction than Type 1. Perhaps that is why you sometimes see paint "bubbles" and minor paint/mold flaws on the Type 2's. They sure didn't get much shaping or painting practice on it. "C" on Cubs hat is often put on backwards. (See below.) No real price penalty on that.

Variations: Besides face types, no real variations worth noting. The Cubs doll is available on a square green base. No premium today for it.

Historical Notes: A set rich in irony. Boston had not very long before signed its first black player when the dolls came out. The crowds had to be 90% to 95% white, with probably 20% to 30% of the players black. So why these?...The black player example is not represented in four franchises: San Francisco, Pittsburgh, Kansas City and Minnesota. This may be evidence that it was a "special order" situation for local vendor...Also, Mays (San Francisco) and Clemente (Pittsburgh) were already on the market...unique hat decals on three dolls: Indians, Colt .45s and Milwaukee Braves...For whatever reason, it seems the entire stock of Washington Senators dolls ended up being for sale everywhere but Washington. Most ended up in Oakland and Buffalo (undoubtedly unsold returns

Cleveland Indians black player, Type 2. Only Indians doll with hat decal. (Jack McGuire)

Chicago Cubs black player, Type 1. Note that it is on a square base. The more common Cubs doll is on a round base.

to East Coast distributor)...The Colt. 45s doll is holding a revolver instead of a ball or bat.

Stumbling Block: Argument could be made that all of them are, so few are their numbers. A set of spectacular rarity. However, even in this situation, one doll stands out. That is the Colt .45s black player. Only six dolls known to exist, and two are repaired. The Yankees is a solid second. I have never seen a mint example of a black Yankees doll.

Want an example? Senators by far the best bet here.

1963-1965 Black Players (all on green bases)

Team	RI	EX	NM	M
Baltimore Orioles	5/6	$400	$600	$900
Boston Red Sox	7/7	$500	$800	$1,200
Chicago Cubs	6/6	$500	$650	$950
Chicago White Sox	6/6	$400	$600	$950
Cincinnati Reds	6/7	$400	$750	$1,200
Cleveland Indians	8/8	$700	$1,000	$1,600
Detroit Tigers	8/8	$500	$650	$1,300
Houston Colt .45s	10/10	$800	$4,000	$8,000
Los Angeles Angels	8/9	$550	$800	$1,400
Los Angeles Dodgers	6/7	$300	$600	$1,100
Milwaukee Braves	7/8	$500	$700	$1,100
New York Mets	8/8	$500	$800	$1,300
New York Yankees	9/9	$700	$1,500	$3,000
Philadelphia Phillies	8/8	$500	$750	$1,100
St. Louis Cardinals	6/7	$350	$450	$900
Washington Senators	2/6	$300	$450	$750

No dolls known for: Kansas City A's, Minnesota Twins, Pittsburgh Pirates and San Francisco Giants.

Red Sox black player, Type 1. At one time, this was one of rarest. A find of about a dozen a few years ago made it "plentiful" for a short time. Although the head is at an angle, it can be fixed. (Jack McGuire)

Once plentiful, this black player Los Angeles Dodgers doll (Type 2) is now a lot tougher to find. (Jack McGuire)

Colt .45s black player, Type 2. This doll holds the record for the highest price ever paid for a doll at $8,400. (Jack McGuire)

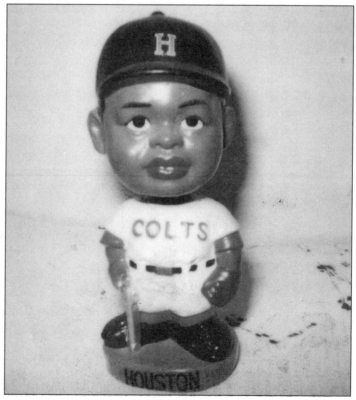

Chapter 5

1963-1965 Green Base

Timeline: Most likely issued 1963-1965.

How to Tell: All dolls on round green bases. "Made in Japan" or "1962" should be visible on bottom of base. If your doll has a piece of felt or a hole there, it is a later date Taiwan doll.

Set Profile: In my mind, the most attractive of baseball sets. Bright colors with staying power. Not difficult set to complete compared to others. All mascots included as before. Colt. 45s doll has revolver in his hand instead of bat. No superstar dolls produced in the green base set, although prototypes of Clemente and Mays are pictured in advertising flyers.

Typical Flaws: A very solidly made doll. Only real weakness seems to be chest decals. They tend to chip.

Significant Variations: 95% of Kansas City A's dolls have light blue hat; 5% dark blue. "Anaheim" variation rare. 90% of Boston dolls have red hat; 10% blue. In the green base set, you have several different hair styles. The only one worth a premium is the "Sideways Hat" variation (see photo), which is worth an extra 15% to 20% premium.

Historical Notes: Last appearance for the Colt .45s, Milwaukee Braves and Los Angeles Angels.

Stumbling Block: Without the variations there are no real stoppers. Cubs has been the traditional key to this set.

Want an example? Los Angeles Angels and Mets probably tied for most common.

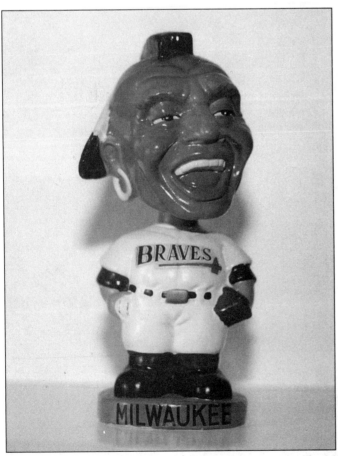

Popular green base Milwaukee Braves mascot head. (Jack McGuire)

Very rare green base "Anaheim" Angels. (Jack McGuire)

1963-1965 Green Base (all on round green bases)

Team	RI	EX	NM	M
Anaheim	8/8	$125	$175	$300
Baltimore Orioles	5/5	$110	$150	$225
Boston Red Sox (red hat)	3/4	$60	$75	$100
Boston Red Sox (blue hat)	8/7	$100	$150	$250
Chicago Cubs	9/6	$200	$350	$450
Chicago White Sox	2/3	$50	$70	$100
Cincinnati Reds	5/5	$100	$140	$190
Cleveland Indians	5/5	$150	$250	$375
Detroit Tigers	5/5	$100	$140	$190
Houston Colt .45s	6/6	$125	$250	$375
Los Angeles Angels	3/3	$70	$100	$135
Los Angeles Dodgers	5/5	$70	$90	$140
Kansas City A's (light blue hat)	6/7	$125	$200	$350
Kansas City A's (dark blue hat)	10/9	$200	$350	$600
Milwaukee Braves	5/6	$150	$250	$375
Minnesota Twins	4/5	$80	$120	$150
New York Mets	2/3	$60	$80	$100
New York Yankees	4/4	$90	$125	$180
Philadelphia Phillies	4/4	$60	$75	$95
Pittsburgh Pirates	6/6	$90	$140	$200
St. Louis Cardinals	4/5	$100	$140	$195
San Francisco Giants	5/5	$70	$90	$130
Washington Senators	4/4	$120	$200	$325

Red and blue hat Red Sox comparison. Note the "curl" and "flat cap" hairstyles. (Jack McGuire)

Some feel the prettiest of all dolls in gem mint is the St. Louis Cardinals green base. (Jack McGuire)

Dark blue light blue KC A's comparison. (Jack McGuire)

Would this doll be subject to gun control? Green base Colt .45s. (Jack McGuire)

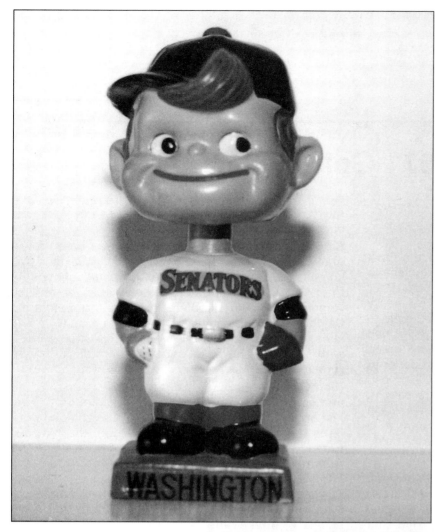

Some leftover white bases were painted green, as was the case with this Washington Senators doll. (Jack McGuire)

Cleveland Indians square green base and regular green base dolls. (author)

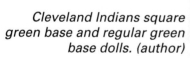

Chapter 6

1966-1971 Gold Base

Timeline: 1966-1971.

How to Tell: All dolls on round gold bases.

Set Profile: The last complete set and by far the most common. Easiest baseball set to complete or obtain an example of. The poorest run as far as quality goes. Poor paint plagues many dolls as well as an inferior (easily damaged) head mold. These problems do not apply to the first run of gold base dolls. These were developed using the old green base dolls, thus the moniker "green base molds." The painting and mold are far superior to regular edition. Can usually tell due to football shaped sticker on bottom of base. Examples that are easy to spot right away include Phillies, Reds and Tigers which still have an embossed chest where subsequent gold bases of these dolls have decals. "Green-base mold" mascot heads are especially striking.

Typical Flaws: Poor (let's call it cheap) paint common on all late run dolls, especially on Mets, Braves, Brewers, and Senators. Heavy varnish on number of dolls. Base decals suffer from chronic chipping. Red Sox doll, for a very strange reason, almost ALWAYS has a messed-up decal on the base, chest or hat. This is a very rare doll with perfect decals.

Significant Variations: Besides the green base molds noted above, there are a good number. Oakland A's comes in white uniform (15% of run) and yellow uniform (85%). The first Senators doll was given an Los Angeles Angel hat complete with halo (no premium). California Angels have three different uniform/hat styles (none commands a premium). Astros comes with an orange hat and "shooting star" decal (3% of run) and plain blue hat and decal (97% of run).

Historical Notes: Only Senators doll with red hat and script "W"...Debut of Texas Rangers doll...The last appearance of the Kansas City A's provided perhaps the most beautiful baseball doll, the famous green and gold uniform...First appearance of Atlanta Braves...First and last appearance of Seattle Pilots...Introduction of 1969 expansion teams, Pilots, Padres, Expos and Royals...Brewers replaced Pilots in 1970. First Brewer doll a Pilots doll with decals removed and temporary "Brewers" paper decals applied.

One of the hobby's most colorful dolls: 1965 Kansas City A's. (Jack McGuire)

Mr. Met is one of the most often repaired dolls, as it was created as a bank. (Jack McGuire)

Stumbling Block: No obvious choice after the Astros variation. Kansas City A's, Pilots and Senators, all with limited runs, are the toughest dolls to acquire. If you want to include the gold base Mays with this set you have just created another huge roadblock. This is one of the rarest dolls in the hobby.

Want an example? Take my yellow uniform A's, Brewers or Expos, please.

1966-1971 Gold Base (all on round gold bases)

Team	RI	EX	NM	M
Atlanta Braves	3/4	$70	$100	$130
Baltimore Orioles	4/4	$90	$130	$160
Boston Red Sox	8/6	$100	$150	$225
California Angels	5/5	$50	$70	$100
Chicago Cubs	5/5	$90	$130	$170
Chicago White Sox	3/3	$50	$70	$90
Cincinnati Reds	5/4	$80	$100	$150
Cleveland Indians	6/5	$125	$225	$325
Detroit Tigers	5/5	$90	$100	$160
Houston Astros (plain decal, blue hat)	2/2	$40	$60	$80
Houston Astros (shooting star decal, red hat)	10/10	$250	$600	$800
Los Angeles Dodgers	5/4	$50	$70	$90
Kansas City A's	8/6	$150	$325	$450
Kansas City Royals	4/4	$50	$70	$110
Milwaukee Brewers	2/1	$30	$50	$70
Minnesota Twins	7/6	$60	$100	$140
Montreal Expos	1/1	$35	$50	$70
New York Mets	3/2	$50	$70	$90
New York Yankees	7/6	$80	$110	$150
Oakland A's (yellow uniform)	1/1	$30	$40	$55
Oakland A's (white uniform)	7/6	$80	$120	$170
Philadelphia Phillies	3/3	$50	$70	$90
Pittsburgh Pirates	5/5	$80	$120	$170
St. Louis Cardinals	4/3	$90	$120	$160

This is the most common Chicago Cubs doll. (Jack McGuire)

Detroit Tigers gold base (with green base mold). Note the embossed "D." Decal chipping on the base would reduce the value by 15%. (Jack McGuire)

Team	RI	EX	NM	M
San Diego Padres	6/5	$70	$90	$120
San Francisco Giants	4/4	$50	$70	$90
Seattle Pilots	7/6	$150	$250	$350
Texas Rangers	6/5	$80	$120	$160
Washington Senators	7/6	$150	$225	$350

Regular gold base Tiger.
Note the decal "D." (Jack McGuire)

This is a gold base Atlanta Braves mascot head (on a green base mold). Note that the head is exactly like green base Milwaukee Braves example in Chapter 5. (Jack McGuire)

Regular gold base Atlanta Braves. (Jack McGuire)

On left: the most common of all dolls—Oakland A's in yellow uniform on gold base; the more scarce white uniform doll at right. (author)

This is a gold base Cincinnati Reds doll on a green base mold. (Jack McGuire)

Here's the regular gold base Cincinnati Reds doll. (Jack McGuire)

The Houston Astros doll with the shooting star decal and red hat on the left is very rare, while the regular blue hat version is pretty common. Note the round base on the shooting star version. (Jack McGuire)

This Washington Senators doll was replaced by the Texas Rangers before the gold base series had ended. (Jack McGuire)

One of biggest error dolls. The Senators doll was given a Los Angeles Angel hat, complete with halo. (Jack McGuire)

Only Japanese-made Rangers doll. (Jack McGuire)

Gold base San Francisco Giants doll. (Jack McGuire)

The Brewers replaced the Pilots suddenly in 1970. The first Brewers doll is a Pilots doll with decals removed and temporary "Brewers" paper decals applied. (Jack McGuire)

Chapter 7

1970-1972 Wedge Base

Timeline: 1970-1972.

How to Tell: All dolls on wedge base. Looks square at first glance but corners are rounded. Face has a "sad" look and is unique to this set.

Set Profile: One of the most mysterious sets. Most likely, a new company that jumped in at, what turned out to be, the end of the game and failed. Only a handful of teams represented and couple (Royals and Cardinals) were not even given their full compliment of decals. All but a couple of these dolls are very rare. Includes Minor League Denver Bears.

Typical Flaws: Astros and Denver Bears doll can have horrible paint on base. The remainder of the teams, discounting Royals and Cardinals, are solid.

Significant Variations: Astros doll comes with an orange hat (75% of run) and blue hat (25%). Keep in mind that this gold wedge base Astro should not be confused with the expensive round gold base "shooting star" Astro in Chapter 6.

Historical Notes: The Denver Bears 1971 American Association championship is noted on the base...Last doll for Cubs was a boy head.

Stumbling Block: Of the "complete" dolls, the Giants is very rare. Cardinals, although ugly, is very scarce. Probably less than 10 surviving Denver Bears.

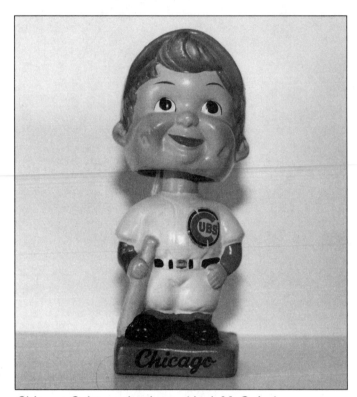

Chicago Cubs wedge base. (Jack McGuire)

1970-1972 Wedge Base

Team	Base Color	RI	EX	NM	M
Boston Red Sox	Gold	8/8	$125	$175	$300
California Angels	White	2/4	$60	$80	$90
Chicago Cubs	Green	7/7	$100	$150	$200
Houston Astros (blue hat)	Gold	3/4	$95	$140	$185
Houston Astros (orange hat)	Gold	3/4	$80	$120	$160
Kansas City Royals	Gold	9/9	$100	$150	$190
Minnesota Twins	Green	3/4	$60	$80	$120
St. Louis Cardinals	Green	9/9	$80	$120	$200
San Francisco Giants	Green	9/9	$150	$200	$350
Denver Bears	Gold	9/9	$200	$400	$600

Chapter 8

Oddball Baseball

Timeline: Throughout 1960s and very early-1970s.

What to Look For: Unusual faces, unique poses, umpires, kissing pairs, derivatives of regular issues.

Profile: Some interesting stuff here. Arguments can be made that square base umpire belongs with white base set and that the Islanders and Mr. Met belong to the gold base. A few dolls were most likely commissioned independently and, judging by remaining examples, not a big hit. A bunch of different umpires are out there. This is a catch-all category that doesn't pretend to cover it all. We will endeavor to point out the most valuable and important of these "free agents."

Typical Flaws: The bank (shake to get coins out) version of Mr. Met is almost always beat up. The most repaired doll in the hobby is Mr. Met. Decals on both Mr. Met dolls are suspect. Base decal, in particular, is often worn away. Beware fake decals here. Islander doll subject to paint flaking. Miniature Astros and Yankees were very poorly done. Weirdo Dodgers, with a ton of detail and mold highlights, are almost always chipped up. Same with the "Drysdale" Dodger.

Significant Variations: I suppose they all are. Some are pictured and that should make it clearer.

Historical Notes: Weirdo Dodger quite possibly the very first baseball bobbing head. Mentioned in 1960 advertising literature...Spokane Indian is merely an Indians white base doll with "Spokane" paper on base.

Stumbling Block: Spokane very rare, as is the "whisk broom" umpire.

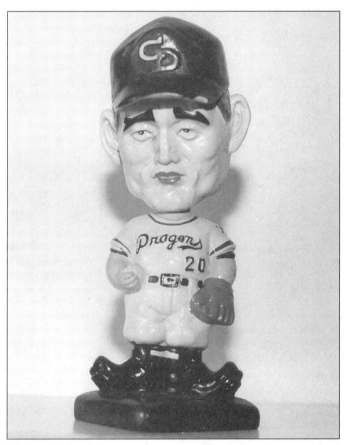

Unique in this country—a Japanese player. (Jack McGuire)

The only umpire to own. (Jack McGuire)

Oddball Baseball

Team	Price Range
1960 rubber doll on wood base (Dodgers, Giants or Braves), each	$50-$80
Boston Red Sox *bank*, green base	$150-$250
Cleveland Indians, mini, green base, (boy head)	$90-$150
Generic Kissing Pair	$30-$50
Hawaii Islander, gold base	$250-$375
Home Run bank, "Bombers"	$75-$125
Houston Astros, round white base with cowboy hat	$150-$250
Houston Astros, mini of previous doll	$200-$350
Houston Astros, round gold base (pale face with *blue* hat and shooting star)	$150-$250
Little Leaguers (several)	$20-$80
Little Leaguer on Globe	$70-$100
Los Angeles Dodgers, "Don Drysdale" set of 3 (Pitcher, Catcher, Hitter), each	$150-$300
Los Angeles Dodgers, green base *bank*	$100-$175
Mr. Met Bank, gold base *bank*	$200-$500
Mr. Met (not a bank)	$250-$550
Minnesota Twins, Kissing Pair Bank	$250-$600
Minnesota Twins, green base with compass between feet	$350-$500
New York Yankees, round white base	$200-$300
New York Yankees, mini of previous doll (sad face, stenciled base)	$250-$400
Spokane, white base	$250-$500
Umpires, various	$100-$500*
Weirdo Los Angeles Dodgers, brown face, (player)	$500-$800
Weirdo Los Angeles Dodgers, white base (5 different dolls), each	$250-$400
Weirdo San Francisco Giants, brown face, (player)	$700-$1,200
Weirdo San Francisco Giants, white base	$300-$600

* *By far most valuable of these is umpire on square green base holding a whisk broom.*

Oddball Dodgers doll. (Jack McGuire)

Mini boy head Cleveland Indians. (Jack McGuire)

Team-issue Astros regular size doll. A mini was also made. (Jack McGuire)

Chapter 9

1960-1961 NFL Square Wood Base

FOOTBALL

Timeline: 1960-1961.

How to Tell: All teams on square wood base. No city decal on base. No wire face mask. NFL teams only. Bases are of various colors.

Set Profile: The first of the professional football dolls. All teams included except the Minnesota Vikings, a later expansion team. There are no decals on helmets of dolls. Embossed team nickname on chest for all teams. Set replaced by *papier mâché* base examples soon after.

Typical Flaws: One of the reasons set was replaced was that the feet sometimes came unglued from the base. If you see one of these dolls standing on only its feet, it is a wood base doll body separated from the base. Not worth much without the base. Other than that, a pretty good mold. Very rear of head susceptible to hair lines.

Significant Variations: Let's look at any dolls that are different than the *papier mâché* twins of the next chapter. The Dallas Cowboys has a totally different helmet and jersey color (blue). The Green Bay doll has a much different green and yellow uniform/helmet color combination. The Los Angeles Rams has a gold colored base instead of blue, although there are blue wood bases, too.

Historical Notes: Set marks the historical debut of the expansion Cowboys...Set was distributed by Los Angeles Rams Merchandising Inc....Rams wood base (gold base) was most likely the first doll of all (the base is larger and thinner than the others).

Stumbling Block: There are some very rare dolls in this set. Packers, Rams and Giants show up only once in awhile.

Want an example? The 49ers shows up a lot. Usually mint in box.

Wood base Philadelphia Eagles doll. Note that the base is thinner than on the regular papier mâché *bases. (Jack McGuire)*

1962 wood base with Falstaff promo. (Jack McGuire)

Very rare Packers wood base. (Jack McGuire)

1960-1961 NFL Square Wood Base (all on square bases)

Team	Base Color	RI	EX	NM	M
Baltimore Colts	Blue	3/3	$50	$70	$100
Chicago Bears	Black	4/4	$60	$80	$110
Cleveland Browns	Brown	7/6	$100	$150	$225
Dallas Cowboys	Light Blue	9/7	$125	$200	$400
Detroit Lions	Silver	4/3	$60	$80	$100
Green Bay Packers	Green	10/9	$150	$250	$400
Los Angeles Rams	Dark Blue	2/2	$50	$60	$80
Los Angeles Rams	Gold	10/9	$150	$275	$450
New York Giants	Blue	8/7	$80	$150	$240
* Philadelphia Eagles	Green	4/4	$90	$120	$160
Pittsburgh Steelers	Black	5/5	$90	$130	$170
** St. Louis Cardinals	Red	8/8	$90	$150	$200
San Francisco 49ers	Red	3/3	$60	$80	$100
Washington Redskins	Maroon	4/5	$120	$140	$190

Most have "1960 Champions" stenciled on base. No premium.

**Some have "Go Go Go For Falstaff" on base, which adds a 20% premium to stated price.*

No doll known for Minnesota.

Rare gold wood base L.A. Rams. (Jack McGuire)

The regular and much more common L.A. Rams doll. (Jack McGuire)

Chapter 10

1961-1963 NFL Square Regular Base

Timeline: 1961-1963.

How to Tell: Same as dolls in Chapter 9, except the regular "one mold" design. The body and base are formed together in *papier mâché*. All dolls on various colored bases.

Set Profile: Much the same as Chapter 9. Decals added on to most teams helmets. Roughly 15% to 20% of these dolls will also have "NFL" embossed/stenciled on the base; about a 20% premium for these examples. You will notice a "Black Player" category in this chapter. In the first attempt to create a "black doll," regular dolls (white) were merely painted dark brown. This was a very crude attempt and may have been done in this country as an experiment. They are all extremely rare. Obviously, it would be fairly easy for anyone to paint a common 1962 square white player dark brown and increase its value 10-fold. For that reason, I suggest strongly you stay away from these. Unless you bought some in the 1980s and know that precise brown color by heart, you should not consider these.

Typical Flaws: Again, the rear of head is where you will see hairline cracks. Decal stripes on helmets can often times be incomplete or chipped.

Significant Variations: None, to speak of. The New York Giants has a chest decal example.

Historical Notes: Debut of expansion Vikings..."NFL" on base probably a symptom of the "war" between the NFL and rival AFL.

Browns 1962 with embossed "NFL" on base. (Jack McGuire)

Stumbling Block: By far the easiest set in all of the sports dolls to complete. No major rarities. Cowboys, Browns and Vikings most in demand.

Want an example? The Rams made up for the shortage of wood base examples by flooding the market with the papier mâché base model.

1961-1963 NFL Square Regular Base

(papier mâché base; base colors same as 1962 NFL Football Wood Base)

Team	RI	EX	NM	M	Black player
Baltimore Colts	3/3	$50	$60	$90	$350
Chicago Bears	4/4	$50	$80	$120	$500
Cleveland Browns	7/6	$100	$140	$190	$900
Dallas Cowboys	7/5	$125	$175	$225	$1,000
Detroit Lions	3/2	$40	$60	$90	$600
Green Bay Packers	5/5	$80	$130	$200	$800
Los Angeles Rams	1/2	$40	$60	$80	$800
Minnesota Vikings	6/6	$100	$140	$180	-
New York Giants	4/4	$60	$80	$120	$800
Philadelphia Eagles	4/4	$60	$80	$120	$350
Pittsburgh Steelers	6/5	$90	$130	$170	$1,000
St. Louis Cardinals	3/3	$50	$65	$80	$700
San Francisco 49ers	3/3	$60	$80	$100	$1,000
Washington Redskins	5/5	$100	$150	$200	$1,500

The paint chip on the base of this Packers doll reduces its value by about 30%. (Jack McGuire)

1962 square black player. (Jack McGuire)

Many of these Colts dolls of these were left over MIB.
(Jack McGuire)

Chapter 11

1960-1961 NFL 15-inch Promo Dolls

Timeline: 1960-1961.

How to Tell: A monster sized doll standing 15-inches tall without any sort of base. Team nicknames on chest via decal. No helmet decal.

Set Profile: All but Vikings (expansion team later) are assumed to exist, although I have never seen or heard of examples for the Giants, Cardinals, Browns and Bears. These were used, it seems, to attract attention to where regular sized dolls were sold. I don't believe you could actually purchase these retail. Only Redskins doll known was found, for example, in the basement of the Washington D.C. Airport. All are extremely rare. Only dolls that show up much are 49ers, Eagles (see historical notes) and Rams. Only NFL teams produced. No AFL.

Typical Flaws: I have never seen a perfect promo. With the immense size of the head, it would be hard not to find something wrong. Damage usually occurs on bottom side, where the head took a massive bounce off shoulders.

Significant Variations: None.

Historical Notes: The NFL crown in 1960 belonged to the Eagles. In 1961, the marketing mavens decided the dolls would sell better if there were some more promo dolls of the Eagles. Hey I have an idea: *Let's change some other teams to Eagles!* So they did. A number of Lions, Packers and other teams dolls were painted green and white on the spot. Instant Eagles! Except there was now no chest decal. *No problem, we'll paint one on!* So they did. Today, if you see an Eagles promo with cursive "Eagles" painted on the chest, you know the story. Only one question remains: What franchise is really under that green and white paint?

Stumbling Blocks: Take your pick.

Want an example? Be at the right place at the right time.

15-inch tall promo Philadelphia Eagles doll at left compared to a regular size doll. (Jack McGuire)

Promo Packers dolls in an extremely rare original box. (Al Polinki)

1960-1961 NFL 15-inch Promo Dolls (not standing on bases)

Team	RI	EX	NM	M
Baltimore Colts	8/10	$800	$1,600	$2,300
Chicago Bears	10/10	$800	$1,500	$3,000
Cleveland Browns	10/10	$1,200	$1,800	$3,000
Dallas Cowboys	9/10	$900	$1,800	$3,000
Detroit Lions	8/10	$800	$1,500	$2,200
Green Bay Packers	7/9	$700	$1,100	$2,000
Los Angeles Rams	5/9	$500	$700	$1,100
New York Giants	10/10	$1,000	$2,000	$3,000
Philadelphia Eagles	3/8	$600	$800	$1,100
Pittsburgh Steelers	10/10	$800	$1,600	$2,800
St. Louis Cardinals	10/10	$800	$1,500	$2,300
San Francisco 49ers	4/8	$750	$1,000	$1,400
Washington Redskins	10/10	$1,800	$2,500	$4,000

No doll seen for Minnesota.

Two promo football dolls.

This promo football doll is the same size as the Falls City Beer bobbing bottle. (author)

Chapter 12

1962-1964 NFL Kissing Pairs

Timeline: 1962-1964.

How to Tell: Football player and majorette. Both 4-1/2-inches tall. Both on gold bases. City designation decal on base of player. Team nickname decal on chest of player. Girl has no decals. Uniforms/markings for both dolls in team colors.

Set Profile: As the name implies, Kissing Pairs were a pair of dolls that, through magnets in lip and cheek, "kissed." All 14 NFL franchises were represented. There are also two AFL pairs that are not included in this set. There were two special pairs that used "mascots" instead of generic "little boys." The Browns (Elf and majorette) and Steelers (Steelworker and majorette) are outstanding examples of bobbing head art, imagination and craftsmanship.

Typical Flaws: The gold flake paint used on base, especially the girl, is prone to extreme chipping. Even gem in box dolls sometimes have this problem. Check base of dolls for repainting. Girl is meant to have a feather in her hat that is often missing. No great price penalty for that currently.

Significant Variations: None.

Historical Notes: During the same time period as the NFL kissing pairs were produced, a great number of generic kissing pairs were out, as well. These represent no team or franchise. They may have "Let's Kiss" or "My Hero" on the base. They are worth little but are sometimes faked to lure the unsuspecting. Many times, the girl is "lifted" to complete a more valuable NFL pair. Usually, however, these generic kissers are on green bases. The NFL pairs are on gold, so difference should be easily noted.

Stumbling Block: The Redskins pair is extremely rare, as is the Browns elf. New York Giants pair is very underrated.

Want an example? Rams dolls found mint in box several years ago in fairly large quantities. Today, it is still the most common. Cowboys comes next.

Very rare kissing pair for the Cleveland Browns. (Jack McGuire)

1962-1964 NFL Kissing Pairs (all on gold bases)

Team	RI	EX	NM	M
Baltimore Colts	8/8	$150	$250	$500
Chicago Bears	8/8	$140	$250	$350
* Cleveland Browns	8/9	$300	$500	$800
Dallas Cowboys	2/4	$125	$175	$250
Detroit Lions	8/8	$200	$350	$550
Green Bay Packers	6/6	$100	$175	$300
Los Angeles Rams	2/3	$80	$140	$180
Minnesota Vikings	8/8	$150	$250	$400
New York Giants	9/8	$150	$300	$600
Philadelphia Eagles	8/8	$150	$250	$450
** Pittsburgh Steelers	5/6	$175	$250	$400
St. Louis Cardinals	6/7	$100	$150	$250
San Francisco 49ers	4/6	$150	$250	$350
Washington Redskins	10/10	$400	$600	$900

* Mascot "Brownie" head, player
** Mascot "Steelworker" head, player

Two AFL examples: Boston Patriots ($200-$500) and Buffalo Bills ($300-$600).

Colts kissing pair. (author)

San Francisco 49ers kissing pair. (Jack McGuire)

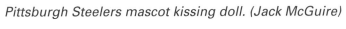

Pittsburgh Steelers mascot kissing doll. (Jack McGuire)

Cowboys kissing pair. (author)

Chapter 13

1961-1966 NFL Toes-Up

Timeline: 1961-1966.

How to Tell: NFL franchises on round various colored bases. Each doll will have his foot and toes pointing up. Thus the "Toes-Up" label.

Set Profile: In this chapter, we probably have at least three sets in one. We will cover, what I believe are the three different types of Toes-Up dolls. However, examples and history of these three are so sketchy and incomplete that it is very difficult to get a handle on it all. Not to mention that the factory seemed to liberally mix and match base/body molds and colors with different heads in the last two sets.

Basic Guidelines: Remember, all have toes up.

Type 1. 1961-1962: Round bases, various base colors that match team color. Ball is held vertically. City decals on base small print. Sometimes find doll with "NFL" on base instead of city. Embossed nickname on chest. "Goofy" face.

Toes-Up Steelers, Type 2. (Jack McGuire)

Type 2. 1963-1965: All on round gold bases. Larger print decals on base. Ball is held vertically. Decal on chest, although some were embossed.

Type 3. 1963-1965: All dolls on round bases of various colors. Balls held horizontally. City on base. Decals on chest.

Type 4: Very similar to Type 1. Various colored bases including a bizarre Steelers doll with a red base. The main difference here is that they are holding the ball horizontally…"Baltimore" on base decal of Colts doll is spelled "Balitmore"…Decals may come in large or small type. All are quite rare.

Again, this is a best educated guess. There are bound to be dolls that don't fit these types.

Typical Flaws: Some Type 1 dolls, the Eagles comes to mind, have paint overruns and sloppy spots. Solid mold, but look for repairs in rear, the weakest spot for all Toes-Up dolls.

Significant Variations: Boy that's tough. A variation might be a totally new set! Probably the type 3 Miami Dolphins and Kansas City Chiefs (See Chapter 20), as they were the only AFL dolls made for that type.

Historical Note: Browns doll comes with famous (non-existent in reality) "CB" helmet decal…Debut of expansion Atlanta Falcons.

Stumbling Block: You can almost take your pick in type 1's. All but a handful are extremely rare.

Want an example? If you are a Rams fan, you are in luck…again!

1961-1966 NFL "Toes-Up" Type

Team	Type 1	Type 2	Type 3	Type 4
Atlanta Falcons	-	-	-	$150-$400
Baltimore Colts	$250-$500	$250-$400	$250-$400	$400-$700
Chicago Bears	$200-$300	$150-$250	$100-$150	$350-$500
Cleveland Browns	$350-$600	$250-$350	$350-$600	$350-$700
Dallas Cowboys	$400-$500	$150-$250	$150-$225	$350-$700
Detroit Lions	$300-$450	$175-$300	$150-$225	$300-$500
Green Bay Packers	$300-$450	$250-$400	$175-$300	$350-$600
Los Angeles Rams	$100-$150	$150-$200	$100-$150	$350-$700
Minnesota Vikings	$300-$450	$150-$250	$150-$250	$350-$700
New York Giants	$300-$500	$200-$350	$75-$135	$300-$600
Philadelphia Eagles	$200-$350	$150-$250	$100-$200	$300-$600
Pittsburgh Steelers	$200-$350	$125-$225	$125-$200	$300-$700 (red base)
St. Louis Cardinals	$200-$350	$150-$300	$250-$400	$150-$300
San Francisco 49ers	$350-$600	$250-$450	$250-$400	$350-$700
Washington Redskins	$400-$700	$150-$300	$150-$300	$500-$800

Toes-Up Bears, Type 2; Toes-Up Packers, Type 1; and Toes-Up Lions, Type 1. (author)

Toes-Up Bears, Type 3. (Jack McGuire)

This Kansas City Chiefs doll, Type 3, is one of two AFL Toes-Up dolls in this set. It's the only doll with number on its chest. (Jack McGuire)

Chapter 14

1962-1964 Black Players Toes-Up

Timeline: 1962-1964.

How to Tell: African-American Players on round gold bases. Toes-Up.

Set Profile: Much like the baseball black players (few made and probably fewer sold). All have African-American features except for the Rams example. Cities on base with decal. Embossed nicknames on chest.

Typical Flaws: Damage likely to occur in rear of head. Check very carefully there on these expensive dolls. Solid mold and design otherwise.

Significant Variation: Rams doll has unique face.

Historical Notes: Again, probably a reflection of the times, but the two scarcest dolls were the two from the South, Wahington and Dallas...The other "Southern" city, St. Louis, is unaccounted for entirely in this set.

Stumbling Block: Combined total of Redskins and Cowboys known to exist would be less than a dozen. Lions, Browns and Colts almost as scarce. No Cardinals doll is known to exist. (See Chapter 15 Historical Notes.)

Want an example? Rams, despite its unique face, and Giants are your best bets.

Lions black player. (Jack McGuire)

1962-1964 Black Players Toes-Up (round base)

Team	RI	EX	NM	M
Baltimore Colts	9/10	$400	$700	$1,200
Chicago Bears	3/7	$200	$350	$450
Cleveland Browns	8/9	$400	$600	$900
Dallas Cowboys	9/10	$350	$600	$1,400
Detroit Lions	8/9	$350	$600	$900
Green Bay Packers	6/9	$400	$700	$900
Los Angeles Rams	2/7	$125	$250	$350
Minnesota Vikings	7/8	$250	$400	$700
New York Giants	3/7	$175	$250	$400
Philadelphia Eagles	3/7	$150	$250	$400
Pittsburgh Steelers	6/8	$200	$400	$650
St. Louis Cardinals (if it exists)	10/10	$400	$1,000	$1,500
San Francisco 49ers	6/8	$250	$400	$700
Washington Redskins	9/10	$800	$1,400	$2,500

San Francisco 49ers black player doll. (author)

Chapter 15

1963-1964 NFL Square Gold Base

Timeline: 1963-1964.

How to Tell: NFL Teams on square gold bases. City name or "NFL" on base. Embossed team nickname on chest.

Set Profile: An obscure, seemingly incomplete group of dolls. Looks like an attempted improvement on the 1962 dolls. Same body style. Heads and helmets more streamlined. Wire face mask on helmet now. Throw into the mix a small group of black players in the same design and you have a confusing pattern of distribution and a sense that these were, in the end, a failure. No one knows if all teams were made, but it looks doubtful.

Typical Flaws: Base chipping hard to avoid with the gold flake paint.

Significant Variations: None.

Historical Notes: It is odd that the St. Louis Cardinals black player in this set is rather common. Could it be the lack of a black player in the Toes-Up set was remedied here? If so, was someone's arm twisted?

Stumbling Block: There is only one known Lions black player.

Want an example? Hard to believe a black player would be the easiest doll in the set, but the Cardinals black player is it. I personally bought one of these (sitting on the very top shelf) in 1981 at the concession stand at Busch Stadium. That doll had sat around for a very long time.

One of few black players from this set that is regularly found. (Jack McGuire)

1963-1964 NFL Square Gold Base

Team	White Player	EX	NM	M	Black Player	EX	NM	M
Baltimore Colts		$125	$200	$300		$300	$400	$600
Chicago Bears		$75	$125	$175		-	-	-
Detroit Lions		$200	$350	$550		$250	$500	$800
Minnesota Vikings		$250	$350	$500		-	-	-
New York Giants		$200	$300	$400		-	-	-
St. Louis Cardinals		$130	$200	$350		$130	$200	$325
Washington Redskins		$125	$225	$350		-	-	-

No dolls seen for: Cleveland, Dallas, Green Bay, Los Angeles, Philadelphia, Pittsburgh and San Francisco.

Some dolls from this set have embossed "NFL" on base, such as this Vikings doll.
(Jack McGuire)

Chapter 16

1965-1967 NFL Gold Round Base

Timeline: 1965-1967.

How to Tell: NFL franchises on round gold bases. Difficult for beginner to tell the difference between these and subsequent 1968 gold bases. Easiest way is to look on the bottom of the base. This doll has a football shaped sticker. The 1968 doll will have a circular decal. This set also has an ever so slightly more mature face and the shoulders are wider. It may also help to look at the arms. This set has the number "00" there. This is not fool proof, however, as a small percentage of 1968 gold bases have the number there, as well.

Set Profile: An extremely well made doll. Most likely the best mold ever. Solid and colorful. I'm sure that these dolls survived spills that would have wrecked others. An NFL set, although there are two AFL examples. Again, a seemingly incomplete set as there seems to be no example for the Rams or 49ers.

Typical Flaws: Although the mold was strong, the decals were weak. A lot of base and helmet decal chips. Steelers doll is almost impossible to find without helmet decal chipping.

Significant Variations: None.

Historical Notes: Debut of expansion New Orleans Saints...Steelers jersey is the famous "yellow apron" style.

Stumbling Block: There are a few tricky dolls (Colts, Browns) but nothing too difficult.

Want an example? The two expansion teams, Saints and Falcons, are extremely well represented.

Famous apron-style Steelers.
(Jack McGuire)

1965-1967
NFL Gold Base

Team	RI	EX	NM	M
Atlanta Falcons	2/2	$45	$60	$80
Baltimore Colts	5/5	$70	$90	$130
Chicago Bears	4/4	$60	$90	$120
Cleveland Browns	5/5	$100	$150	$225
Dallas Cowboys	4/4	$90	$140	$200
Detroit Lions	5/5	$60	$80	$100
Green Bay Packers	3/4	$90	$140	$180
Minnesota Vikings	4/4	$80	$130	$190
New Orleans Saints	2/2	$40	$60	$80
New York Giants	6/5	$70	$90	$140
Philadelphia Eagles	4/4	$70	$90	$130
Pittsburgh Steelers	4/5	$90	$130	$170
Washington Redskins	5/5	$100	$150	$225

No doll seen for Los Angeles or San Francisco.

Chapter 17

1965-1967 NFL Gold Round Base/Realistic Face

Timeline: 1965-1967.

How to Tell: NFL franchises on a gold round base. Each doll has a realistic or "man" face instead of the boy head. Molded ear pads on helmet.

Set Profile: Unique in the face style. Another incomplete set, as no examples of the Rams, Steelers, Giants or 49ers has ever been seen. Probably another special order, as quite a few teams are scarce. Reasoning behind creation of set remains a question. It was never repeated in any set, any sport.

Typical Flaws: Like the 1965 gold base set, this one is remarkably well done. Solid mold and good paint. Only exception being the Saints doll which suffers from paint flaking. Base decals are also prone to rubbing and chipping.

Significant Variations: None.

Historical Notes: This man face doll must have appealed to the concessionaire in Louisiana, as not only were the Saints purchased in huge numbers but college examples of Tulane and LSU also show up regularly.

Stumbling Block: Good luck in finding a Redskins, Colts or Cowboys.

Want an example? I would say that there are as many New Orleans Saints dolls out there as there are the rest of the teams combined.

Realistic or "man" face Detroit Lions doll. (Jack McGuire)

1965-1967 NFL Gold Round Base/Realistic Face

Team	RI	EX	NM	M
Atlanta Falcons	6/5	$70	$90	$120
Baltimore Colts	9/9	$200	$350	$600
Chicago Bears	6/6	$100	$140	$180
Cleveland Browns	7/8	$150	$325	$450
Dallas Cowboys	9/10	$200	$400	$600
Detroit Lions	8/8	$150	$225	$325
Green Bay Packers	5/5	$100	$175	$250
Minnesota Vikings	8/8	$200	$300	$450
New Orleans Saints	1/1	$30	$50	$70
Philadelphia Eagles	7/7	$125	$225	$325
St. Louis Cardinals	6/6	$75	$100	$140
Washington Redskins	10/10	$300	$500	$800

No dolls seen for: Los Angeles, New York Giants, Pittsburgh or San Francisco.

Realistic or "man" face Chicago Bears doll. (Jack McGuire)

Chapter 18

1968-1970 NFL/AFL Gold Round Base

Timeline: 1968-1970.

How to Tell: All dolls on gold round bases. See Chapter 16 to tell difference between 1965 gold and 1968 gold. NFL stickers between feet.

Set Profile: Often known as the "Merger Set," as it is the first and only football set that includes all NFL and previous AFL franchises. Also, it's the largest of all sports sets with 26 teams. Like the gold base baseball, a set that was produced in great numbers and since it was over the last set, a decent number of unsold dolls were left over for today's collector. The first run of this model/set had the former AFL franchises with an AFL sticker between feet. This group covered in Chapter 20.

Typical Flaws: Very weak/thin mold. Almost impossible to find this doll without a hairline or two in the rear of the head. Even mint in box dolls are victim. If the doll is mishandled in any way, the results are not pretty. The Saints doll almost always has paint peeling (over-

Gold base Baltimore Colts. (Jack McGuire)

Gold base Minnesota Vikings. (Jack McGuire)

baked). The Colts, Browns, Boston Patriots and Jets are other teams, for whatever reason, seemed to have a mold that lent itself to paint peeling and chipping, hairlines, and generally poor overall appearance. There are nice examples of these dolls out there but you have to look harder.

Significant Variations: This set is the king of variations. In fact, I believe every team had two different jersey colors. Usually, it's only a shade difference, so I won't list all. The variations with price premium are listed. For example, the Falcons doll in this set usually has a red jersey. If you have one with a black (don't get confused with 1965 gold Falcon!) jersey you have a doll that will bring 30% more in corresponding grade. You will notice that the Redskins has four variations listed by helmet style alone. Keep in mind you can mix and match jersey colors (yellow and maroon) here too if you want to list them all. The point is, with so many variations, which one isn't a variation? Price given is a composite of all variations. You may get more if you find the right person needing the right variation.

Historical Notes: First and last appearance for the Bengals...Boston Patriots replaced by New England Patriots about a quarter way through run...Cleveland is represented with AFL sticker on feet. I have never seen Baltimore and Pittsburgh AFL examples (other two NFL teams that "transferred")...Last of the *papier mâché* "Made in Japan" football dolls.

Stumbling Block: If you toss out variations, not a difficult set to complete. Dolphins, Bills, Browns and, lately, Packers usually a bit of a challenge.

Want an example? At a flea market in Pennsylvania, a few years back, thousands of mint in box Chiefs, Cardinals, Lions and Bengals were found. They were not exactly rare before that find.

Gold base Buffalo Bills. (Jack McGuire)

One of five styles of Redskins gold base dolls. (Jack McGuire)

1968-1970 NFL/AFL Gold Round Base "Merger Series"

Team	RI	EX	NM	M	Variation—Premium
Atlanta Falcons	3/3	$50	$70	$90	Black jersey—30%
Baltimore Colts	5/4	$60	$90	$130	-
Boston Patriots	5/5	$70	$90	$130	-
Buffalo Bills	5/5	$100	$140	$180	-
Chicago Bears	4/4	$50	$70	$90	-
Cincinnati Bengals	2/2	$30	$50	$70	-
Cleveland Browns	6/5	$90	$140	$180	-
Dallas Cowboys	5/5	$90	$130	$180	White helmet—20%
Denver Broncos	6/5	$90	$130	$180	Blue jersey—50%
Detroit Lions	2/2	$30	$45	$60	-
Green Bay Packers	5/5	$90	$140	$190	-
Houston Oilers	2/2	$30	$50	$70	Blue helmet—100%
Kansas City Chiefs	2/2	$30	$50	$70	-
Los Angeles Rams	3/3	$40	$60	$90	Gold horns—100%
Miami Dolphins	6/6	$100	$150	$190	-

Rare Broncos with blue jersey. (Jack McGuire)

Common Broncos with red jersey. (Jack McGuire)

Team	RI	EX	NM	M	Variation—Premium
Minnesota Vikings	5/5	$100	$150	$190	-
New England Patriots	4/4	$60	$90	$110	-
New Orleans Saints	2/2	$40	$55	$70	Black helmet—100%
New York Giants	3/3	$40	$60	$80	-
New York Jets	5/5	$70	$90	$130	-
Oakland Raiders	5/5	$90	$125	$160	-
Philadelphia Eagles	5/5	$70	$90	$130	Green wings—20%
Pittsburgh Steelers	5/5	$80	$130	$170	-
St. Louis Cardinals	2/2	$30	$50	$70	-
San Diego Chargers	3/3	$50	$60	$100	-
San Francisco 49ers	6/5	$100	$130	$180	White helmet—100%
Washington Redskins	5/5	$100	$140	$200	Yellow helmet "R"
					Maroon helmet "R"
					Maroon helmet "Chief"
					Maroon helmet "Spear"

Ultra rare Broncos with orange helmet and jersey and AFL sticker. (Jack McGuire)

Gold base Saints, Cowboys, Packers and Falcons (the Falcons doll has the harder to find black jersey). (author)

Chapter 19

1961-1962 AFL Round Base/Toes-Up

Timeline: 1961-1962.

How to Tell: All dolls on round bases of various colors. All dolls with "Toes-Up" feature. Wire face masks. Ball held horizontally. "American Football League" sticker bottom of base.

Set Profile: Original AFL set most likely issued in the league's second season—a season that saw the Raiders at a high school field and the New York Titans at the Polo Grounds. Few fans, few dolls sold. An historical and romantic set that is extremely underpriced to me.

Typical Flaws: Other than wear and tear for an almost 40-year-old doll, there are no real problem areas. You will run into situations with this sets' decals. In the best case, the doll will have the nickname on the chest and the city decal on the base. In other cases, you will see nickname on base and no city. Or city on base and no chest nickname decal. I would hold out for the best case if I were you, but this doesn't make the decal-challenged dolls any less legitimate.

Significant Variations: None.

Very rare New York Titans. (Jack McGuire)

Historical Notes: Only examples of Dallas Texans (Chiefs) and New York Titans (Jets)...Some great helmet decals for Oilers (gushing derrick) Texans (map of Texas) and Patriots (three-cornered hat)...Original colors for Broncos (brown and gold); Raiders (black and gold); and Bills (blue and silver)...Set came one year too late for Los Angeles Chargers, as the as San Diego Chargers doll proves.

Stumbling Block: The Titans and Texans bring the most, but the Raiders might be the rarest. All dolls in this set are rare.

Want an example? You would be lucky to find any, but Broncos and Patriots seem most likely.

1961-1962 AFL Round Base/Toes-Up

Team	Base Color	RI	EX	NM	M
Boston Patriots	Blue	7/7	$200	$350	$600
Buffalo Bills	Silver	5/7	$240	$330	$550
Dallas Texans	Gold	8/9	$300	$550	$800
Denver Broncos	Gold	7/8	$250	$400	$700
Houston Oilers	White	9/9	$250	$400	$700
New York Titans	Blue	10/9	$400	$700	$1,200
Oakland Raiders	Gold	8/9	$300	$450	$750
San Diego Chargers	Blue	8/8	$225	$325	$500

Oakland Raiders doll from 1961-1962 AFL set. (Jack McGuire)

1961-1963 NHL Square Base (left) and 1961-1963 NHL Miniature (right) New York Rangers.

1961-1963 Canadian High Skates Miniature, Boston Bruins.

1967-1968 NHL Gold Base, Los Angeles Kings.

Minor League Hockey, Baltimore Clippers.

1960-1961 Square Color Base, Pittsburgh Pirates mascot head

1960-1961 Square Wood Base, San Francisco Giants boy head.

1961-1962 White Base Miniature, Boston Red Sox boy head.

1961-1962 White Base Miniature Mantle and Maris.

1961-1962 Green Base Miniature, Cleveland Indians mascot head.

1961-1963 White Base, Pittsburgh Pirates mascot head.

1961-1963 White Base, Anaheim Angels boy head.

1961-1963 Square and Round White Base Mantles.

1961-1963 White Base Mays, light and dark faces.

1961-1963 White Base Maris.

1961-1963 White Base Clemente.

Baseball

1963-1965 Black Player, Los Angeles Dodgers "Little Boy Face."

1963-1965 Black Player, Cleveland Indians "Realistic Face."

1963-1965 Green Base, St. Louis Cardinals mascot head (some say this is the finest bobbing head ever made).

1963-1965 Square Green Base, Washington Senators boy head.

1963-1965 Green Base, Houston Colt .45s with Colt .45 Pistol.

1963-1965 Green Base Kansas City A's with light blue hat and dark blue hat, both featuring sideways hats.

1963-1965 Green Base Boston Red Sox with red hat and blue hat.

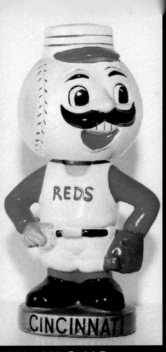

1968-1971 Gold Base,
Detroit Tigers mascot head.

1966-1967 Gold Base,
Cincinnati Reds mascot
head.

1966-1971 Gold Base,
Chicago Cubs mascot head.

1971 Gold Base, Texas
Rangers (only Japan-made
Rangers doll).

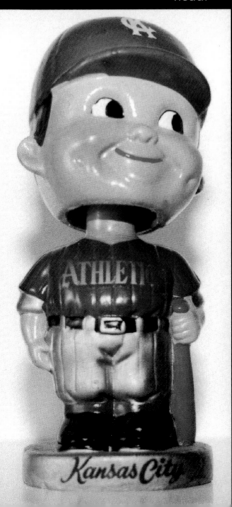

1963-1964 NFL Square Gold Base, Minnesota Vikings.

1960-1961 NFL Square Wood Base, St. Louis Cardinals.

1962 NFL Square Regular Base, Baltimore Colts black player.

1965-1967 NFL "Realistic Face" Chicago Bears.

1961-1966 NFL Toes-Up, Pittsburgh Steelers.

1962-1964 Black Players Toes-Up, Detroit Lions.

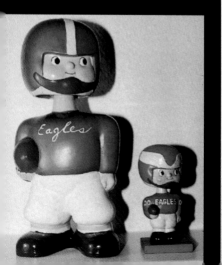

1965-1967 NFL Gold Base, Pittsburgh Steelers.

1968-1970 NFL/AFL Gold Round Base, Washington Redskins.

1961-1962 AFL Round Base/Toes-Up, Oakland Raiders.

1965-1966 AFL Gold Base, Houston Oilers.

1961-1965 Canadian Football.

College, Florida Gators.

College, Hula Bowl.

College, Baylor Bears.

Personalities

Frankenstein

Dick Tracy

Elmer Fudd

Red Goose Shoes

Roy Rogers

Smokey Bear

John Kennedy

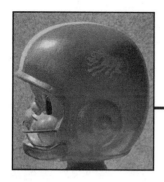

Chapter 20

1965-1966 AFL Gold Base/Ear Pads & Other AFL

Timeline: 1965-1966.

How to Tell: This chapter will focus on the ear pads set. Descriptions of the other AFL dolls are mentioned. All are on round gold bases. Mold is distinctive due to molded ear pads on helmet. Face unique.

Set Profile: The second and last "purely" AFL set. Colorful and historic, a great football set.

Typical Flaws: Base decals are prone to chipping. Helmet and chest decals prone to fading, chipping and wear. Solid mold.

Significant Variations: Only one worth noting is the Redskins example. Only NFL team to appear in this design.

Historical Notes: First doll for Dolphins, Chiefs, and Jets...Broncos doll with "Silly Horse" helmet decal.

Stumbling Block: No easy doll here. Broncos, however, is one of the hobby's ultra rarities. Only a handful known to exist.

Want an example? Try the Chiefs, but no guarantees.

1965-1966 AFL Gold Base/Ear Pads

Team	RI	EX	NM	M
Boston Patriots	7/7	$150	$250	$350
Buffalo Bills	7/7	$150	$250	$375
Denver Broncos	10/10	$500	$900	$1,300
Kansas City Chiefs	7/7	$150	$225	$325
Houston Oilers	9/8	$200	$350	$450
Miami Dolphins	7/7	$175	$250	$450

Houston Oilers: One of two AFL dolls in the NFL dominated 1965 gold set. (Jack McGuire)

Buffalo Bills 1968 gold base with sticker on base. (Jack McGuire)

Team	RI	EX	NM	M
New York Jets	9/9	$250	$400	$700
Oakland Raiders	8/8	$250	$350	$500
San Diego Chargers	8/8	$200	$300	$400
Washington Redskins (NFL)	8/8	$300	$400	$500

1965 AFL Gold Base

Team	EX	NM	M
Denver Broncos	$150	$225	$300
Houston Oilers	$125	$175	$225

1965 AFL Toes-Up

Team	EX	NM	M
Miami Dolphins	$175	$250	$350
Kansas City Chiefs (decal #55 on back of shirt)	$130	$200	$325

1968 Gold Bases AFL (sticker on base)

Team	EX	NM	M
Boston Patriots	$100	$140	$180
Buffalo Bills	$100	$150	$210
Cleveland Browns	$140	$250	$330
Denver Broncos (unique orange helmet)	$170	$300	$500
Houston Oilers	$70	$90	$110
Kansas City Chiefs	$50	$70	$90
Miami Dolphins	$150	$200	$250
New York Jets	$80	$120	$150
Oakland Raiders	$100	$140	$180
San Diego Chargers	$70	$90	$120

No dolls seen for: Cincinnati or New England.

Side view showing molded ear pads on Broncos helmet. (Jack McGuire)

The toughest dolls in the "ear pad" set, the Denver Broncos. (Jack McGuire)

Chapter 21

1961-1965 Canadian Football

Timeline: 1961-1965.

How to Tell: All dolls on square bases regular set. CFL franchises only. Dolls can be small size (5 inches) or regular size (6-1/2 inches). No face masks. Mascot dolls are flat to surface (snake-like) with mascot head hooked (no spring) to neck area.

Set Profile: Regular size CFL dolls a twin to 1962 square base NFL dolls. Including a wood base and *papier mâché* base variation. No premium either way here. No city on base. Nickname on chest. Smaller examples will have city or province on base. Does not look like distribution was anywhere but Canada. Mascot heads are extremely rare and not a whole lot is known.

Typical Flaws: See Chapter 10.

Significant Variations: Can find "Vancouver" or "B.C." on Lions dolls. Roughriders doll can sometimes be found with "Regina."

Historical Notes: Does not seem like the dolls continued to be produced after 1965.

Stumbling Block: Montreal has always been difficult to find. Perhaps the nodder lacked a little *savoir faire*, if you know what I mean.

Want an example? None of these ever found in quantity. I imagine it would depend on how close you are to certain points in Canada.

Very rare CFL mascot doll: B.C. Lions. (Jack McGuire)

1961-1965 Canadian Football

Team	Regular Size	Small	Mascot
BC Lions (lion)	$125-$200	$125-$200	$350-$500
Calgary (horse)	$125-$200	$125-$200	$350-$500
Hamilton	$125-$200	$125-$200	-
Montreal (bird)	$150-$250	$125-$200	$350-$600
Saskatchewan	$125-$200	$125-$200	-
Toronto Maple Leafs	$125-$200	$125-$200	-
Winnipeg	$125-$200	$125-$200	-

CFL Calgary Stampeeders. (Jack McGuire)

Regular and smaller size CFL Eskimos dolls. (Jack McGuire)

Chapter 22

1961-1968 College Football & Oddball Football

Timeline: 1961-1968.

How to Tell: University and college football players are almost always on a round green base. There are some on a square base and some on a round gold base. Beware! There are hundreds of bogus gold base dolls (see Historical Notes). There is also a handful of college mascot heads. Inside the college football doll "set," you will find every (except kissing pairs) pro football style mentioned in the last 13 chapters!

Set Profile: Most college dolls are "Toes-Up." There are at least three different mold styles:

Type 1. Colored bases "Bobbie style"

Type 2. Green base "long shoulder pads"

Type 3. Green base "short shoulder pads"

Only Type 1 is recognizably different and may bring more than prices listed. Some schools came out in multiple designs, including very well done mascot heads. Those are noted in the guide. This listing does not pretend to be complete. There can certainly be a school out there that I have not seen. Readers are welcome to let us know on these. Prices, unless noted, are a composite of all three types.

Typical Flaws: See Chapter 13.

Significant Variations: See guide. The miniatures are the most spectacular.

Historical Notes: Along with the college dolls came "generics." Identical in every respect to the valuable dolls listed, except they had no decals applied at the

Oregon "Webfoots" doll. (Jack McGuire)

One of five colors the All American doll can be found in. (Jack McGuire)

factory. Evidently these dolls, in a variety of color combinations, were to be sold to high schools, smaller colleges, etc., for fund-raising. I don't think it worked out. Thousands of these dolls were left over. They were mostly gold base, but some green base Toes-Up. One dealer, in 1992, bought hundreds of generic gold base dolls and applied fake decals and paint, then sold them as authentic. They are still around. Stay away from gold base college football dolls if you can peel the decal off! There were only a few gold base college football teams, so almost any is liable to be fake...The green base Toes-Up generics have been turned into fakes through stenciling. No college football doll, on a green base, ever had stenciling on the base *and* chest!

Stumbling Block: Of all dolls listed, probably the Washington State cougar head and LSU tiger head are the two most spectacular rarities.

Want an example? When living in Kansas in 1985, I bought 40 KSU green bases at a flea market in Wichita for $2 each. The lady said she had more, but that was enough for me. Well, she had 1,400 more, as it turned out! All mint in the box.

This Utah State Aggies doll is one of three known miniature college football dolls. (Jack McGuire)

Most gold base college football dolls are fake. This Florida Gators doll is one of the few real ones (Wisconsin, Army, Navy and Notre Dame are the others). This doll also comes with "NFL" sticker between the feet. (Jack McGuire)

This UCLA Bruins doll is also from about 1959 and sports a felt helmet. (Jack McGuire)

1961-1968 College Football

Team	Round Green Base	Other
Air Force	$125-$175	Mini—$70-$150
Alabama	$175-$300	-
Arizona State	-	Devil head—$300-$500
Arkansas	$175-$300	-
Army	$90-$125	Gold base—$70-$100
Bakersfield (JC)	$75-$125	-
Baylor	$125-$175	Bear head—$300-$600
Boston College	$175-$300	-
BYU	$200-$300	-
Bowling Green	$150-$250	-
Bradley	$150-$300	-
Brown	$140-$225	-
Bucknell	$150-$300	-
Buffalo	$110-$160	-
Cal	$150-$250	Bear head—$250-$400
Clemson	$200-$300	-
Coast Guard	$175-$250	-
Colgate	$175-$300	-
Colorado	$200-$350	-

College mascot head for North Texas State, very rare. (Bruce Stjernstrom)

College mascot head for Baylor, very rare. (Bruce Stjernstrom)

Team	Round Green Base	Other
Columbia	$140-$225	-
Cornell	$160-$260	-
Dartmouth	$140-$225	-
Delaware	$175-$300	-
Drake	$150-$250	-
Duke	$225-$350	-
Florida	$200-$350	Gold base—$75-$150
Fresno St.	$125-$200	-
Georgia	$175-$300	-
Georgia Tech	$150-$250	-
Harvard	$175-$300	-
Holy Cross	$150-$300	-
Illinois	$150-$300	Red base—$250-$350
Indiana	$150-$300	Red base—$250-$400
Iowa	$150-$300	Old gold base—$250-$400
Iowa St.	$150-$300	-
Kansas (Jayhawkers!)	$150-$300	-
Kansas St.	$100-$175	Green base, NO Toes-Up—$40-$50
Kent St.	$150-$250	-
Kentucky	$200-$350	-
Lafayette	$125-$175	-

College football mascot for Stanford Indians. (Jack McGuire)

Rare Pacific Tigers college mascot. (Jack McGuire)

Team	Round Green Base	Other
Lehigh	$125-$175	-
LSU	$150-$300	Man face—$125-$175
	Tiger head—$600-$800	
Maine	$100-$160	-
Maryland	$200-$350	-
Massilon High	$250-$400	-
Miami (FL)	$250-$350	-
Michigan	$250-$400	Blue base—$300-$450
		Square base—$400-$800
Michigan St.	$175-$250	Old Green base—$200-$350
Minnesota	$90-$150	Maroon base—$200-$350
Ole Miss	$200-$350	-
Mississippi St.	$175-$275	-
Missouri	$250-$400	-
Navy	$100-$150	Gold base—$80-$120
Nebraska	$250-$450	-
North Carolina	$225-$350	-
NC State	$200-$325	-
North Texas	-	Eagle head—$300-$500
Northwestern	$200-$300	Blue base—$200-$300
Notre Dame	$100-$175	Sq. blue base/Shamrock—$300-$500
	Gold "man" face—$90-$150	
	Gold and ear pads—$70-$125	

This California example is a typical college Toes-Up doll. (Jack McGuire)

Square base college football. (Jack McGuire)

Team	Round Green Base	Other
Michigan	$250-$400	Blue base—$300-$450
Michigan St.	$175-$250	Green base—$200-$350
Minnesota	$90-$150	Maroon base—$200-$350
Ole Miss	$200-$350	-
Mississippi St.	$175-$275	-
Missouri	$250-$400	-
Navy	$100-$150	Gold base—$80-$120
North Carolina	$225-$350	-
NC State	$200-$325	-
North Texas	-	Eagle head—$300-$500
Northwestern	$200-$300	Blue base—$200-$300
Notre Dame	$100-$175	Square blue base—$300-$500
	Gold "man" face—$90-$150	
	Gold and ear pads—$70-$125	
Ohio State	$225-$350	Red base—$250-$400
Ohio University	$125-$175	-
Oklahoma	$250-$400	-
Oregon	$225-$350	-
Oregon St. (OSC)	$150-$250	-
Pacific	-	Tiger head—$300-$500
Penn St.	$250-$400	No Base w/pin—$150-$250

White base Toes-Up Purdue. (Jack McGuire)

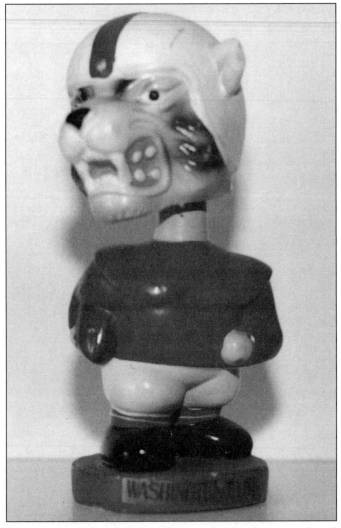

Ultra rare Washington State cougar mascot head. (Jack McGuire)

Team	Round Green Base	Other
Penn	-	Nice rubber version—$70
Pittsburgh	$175-$250	-
Princeton	$125-$175	-
Purdue	$200-$350	Old gold base—$150-$250
Rice	$175-$250	-
Rutgers	$125-$200	-
San Jose St.	$175-$300	-
St. Johns	-	Red base—$200-$400
Southern Cal	$90-$140	-
South Illinois	$150-$240	-
SMU	$125-$200	-
Southern Miss	-	Round white—$100-$150
Stanford	-	Indian head—$400-$850
Syracuse	$175-$275	-
Tennessee	$250-$400	Orange base—$200-$500
Texas	$200-$400	Steer head—$300-$700
Texas A&M	$200-$350	-
TCU	$150-$250	-
Texas Tech	$150-$300	-
Toledo	$125-$250	-
Tufts	$140-$300	-
Tulane	$150-$250	Man face—$100-$175
UCLA	$125-$225	-
Utah	-	Miniature—$200-$300

The Hula Bowl was the only college bowl game with a doll. (Jack McGuire)

Texas mascot doll. (Jack McGuire)

Team	Round Green Base		Other
Vanderbilt	$135-$200		White base—$80-$140
Virginia	$160-$250		-
VMI	$140-$275		-
Virginia Tech	$140-$250		-
Wake Forest	$175-$300		White base—$150-$250
Washington	$130-$225		Purple base—$120-$150
Washington St.	$140-$250		Cougar head—$400-$800
Waynesburg	$130-$200		-
William & Mary	$175-$300		-
Wisconsin	$200-$450		Orange square—$150-$350
	Red round—$300-$600		
	Gold round—$90-$150		
Yale	$180-$350		

There have been no dolls seen for the following colleges: Arizona, Auburn, Colorado St., Florida St., Hawaii, Houston, Louisville, Memphis St., Miami (OH), Nevada, New Mexico, Oklahoma State, San Diego St., South Carolina, Temple, Texas Western, Tulsa, West Virginia and Wyoming.

First- (right) and second-issue (left) Northwestern dolls. (Jack McGuire)

The Air Force Academy doll in regular size is rarer than the mini. (Jack McGuire)

Early Big 10 dolls: Wisconsin Badgers and Michigan Wolverines. (author)

Notre Dame green base doll. (author)

Oddball Football

Item	Price Range
"All Star" Banks (5 different colors), each	$60-$90
Generic Kissing Pair	$30-$40
Generic Player	$20-$30
Jets Bank	$100-$130
Los Angeles Rams, felt helmet, square wood base, 1959	$70-$90
New York Giants, "pin on chest"	$100-$130
Oakland Raiders Square Base	$500-$700
San Diego Chargers Square Green	$100-$125
"Touchdown" Bank	$60-$80
UCLA Bruins, felt helmet, square wood base, 1959	$70-$90

Prototype Washington Redskins doll. Examples are also known for the Detroit Lions and San Francisco 49ers. (Jack McGuire)

Very rare Oakland Raiders square base. (Jack McGuire)

One of very first dolls, this one was featured in a 1959 L.A. Rams program. The helmet is made of felt. (Jack McGuire)

Chapter 23

1961-1963 NHL Square Base

HOCKEY

Timeline: 1961-1963.

How to Tell: Original six NHL franchises on square base of various colors. City decal on base. Nickname decal on chest.

Set Profile: Obviously a very short set but a bit of a challenge. Doubt as many hockey dolls produced as baseball and football. Blackhawks and Canadiens found in quantity a few years back. Blackhawks, at time, was the rarest doll, so the newly found dolls (in the Blackhawks' case) were quickly absorbed.

Typical Flaws: A well made doll. Only complaint being that the base seems to chip, especially on the base corners. Paint on hair chips, too. Perhaps the hair chips are more noticeable, as this is the only set not with a hat or helmet.

Significant Variations: None.

Historical Notes: Doesn't seem that long ago that there were only six NHL franchises...Looks as if these were sold strictly as a stadium vendor item.

Stumbling Block: Boston Bruins. Since day one in the hobby this doll has reigned supreme. A very scarce doll considering such a short set.

Want an example? *Viva le dolls!* It's the Canadiens, by far.

Comparison of the regular size New York Rangers and ultra rare mini. (Jack McGuire)

1961-1963 NHL Square Base

Team	Base Color	RI	EX	NM	M
Boston Bruins	Yellow/gold	9/8	$300	$425	$600
Chicago Blackhawks	Red	6/6	$125	$175	$225
Detroit Redwings	Red	6/6	$140	$175	$225
Montreal Canadiens	Blue	3/4	$70	$90	$125
New York Rangers	Blue	4/4	$100	$140	$190
Toronto Maple Leafs	Blue	5/5	$80	$140	$190

The Boston Bruins doll is the key to the regular 1962 set. (Jack McGuire)

Chapter 24

1961-1963 NHL Miniature

Timeline: 1961-1963.

How to Tell: 4 inches high on square base. Color same as regular size. City name stenciled on base. Nickname decal on chest.

Set Profile: Most likely issued as companion set to regular size set. Identical teams and color combinations. Face much different and not for the better. Three dolls from this set have the distinction, with out a doubt, of being the most common bobbing head dolls.

Typical Flaws: The face of the doll often has unfinished areas. Sloppy paint throughout. Stenciling on base was done, to be kind, erratically.

Significant Variations: Some, well a lot, of Maple Leaf dolls have Red Wing decal on chest.

Historical Notes: Once upon a time, all hockey miniatures were rare. They were virtually unknown in the hobby until around 1986-1987. Any example would bring $450, easy. Then the roof caved in. In late-1989, thousands of mint in the box Leafs, Canadiens and Red Wings were found. A short time later, thousands of Blackhawks and Bruins. A short time after that, more Leafs, Canadiens, and Red Wings. Never has the hobby seen such a sight. A doll that was $450 six months ago was now selling for $10-$15 wholesale. Today it seems that all of the dolls have finally been absorbed.

Stumbling Block: Let's see, five teams were found in huge quantities, there were only six teams. That leaves one out, the Rangers. The absurdity of doll science is best pointed out here. Inside a six-team set

Very common mini Boston Bruins doll. (Jack McGuire)

where five were found in massive quantities you have one of the rarest dolls in the doll universe. Why this is so I can't say. Certainly no quantities larger than one have turned up in the last 20 years. A note of caution. A doll artist took a number of Leafs dolls and repainted them into Rangers. It was good work and he was kind enough to leave a tell tale sign as well. Any miniature Rangers doll that has a *decal* on the base is not legit.

Want an example? Don't want to be redundant.

1961-1963 NHL Miniature (same base colors as 1962 NHL Square Base)

Team	RI	EX	NM	M
Boston Bruins	2/2	$20	$40	$60
Chicago Blackhawks	2/2	$25	$40	$60
Detroit Redwings	1/1	$15	$30	$50
Montreal Canadiens	1/1	$15	$30	$50
* New York Rangers	10/10	$350	$900	$1,600
** Toronto Maple Leafs	1/1	$15	$30	$50

* Beware of fakes.
** Some have Red Wings decal on chest. No premium.

Toronto mini with error Detroit decal.

Chapter 25

1961-1963 Canadian "High Skates"

Timeline: 1961-1963.

How to Tell: Comes in two sizes, regular 6-1/2 inches and small 5 inches. Set probably should have been called "High Blade" (see photo), as that is what really sets this set apart from its 1962 American regular size cousin. Slightly different face style. (There is no U.S. set to compare to the high skates small size.) Blackhawks in this set comes on a light blue base.

Set Profile: A set seemingly made for Canada, although I know some where sold in the United States. Original six NHL teams. Small size set unique, but follows same color patterns (with the exception of the Blackhawks) as all NHL square base hockey.

Typical Flaws: See Chapter 24.

Significant Variations: None.

Stumbling Block: All high skates are rare in the United States. In the large size, I haven't seen many Detroit dolls. In the smaller size, I guess Montreal. All are rare, and I had been in the hobby 12 years before I knew they existed.

Want an example? Blackhawks and Canadiens seem to show up in the regular size every two or three years.

Comparison (from left): regular size NHL Square Base, Canadian miniature "High Skates" and NHL Miniature. (author)

1962 NHL "High Skates" (all rare)

Team	Base Color	RI	Price Range
Boston Bruins	Yellow/Gold	8/9	$250-$600
Chicago Blackhawks	Light Blue	8/9	$225-$400
Detroit Redwings	Red	9/9	$275-$450
Montreal Canadiens	Red	7/7	$175-$275
New York Rangers	Blue	8/8	$225-$375
Toronto Maple Leafs	Blue	8/8	$200-$350

1962 Smaller "High Skates" (same color bases, extremely rare)

Team	Price Range
Boston Bruins	$300-$450
Chicago Blackhawks	$250-$400
Detroit Redwings	$300-$450
Montreal Canadiens	$350-$500
New York Rangers	$300-$450
Toronto Maple Leafs	$300-$450

High Skates. (author)

High Skates. (author)

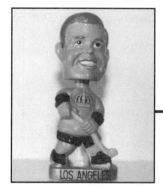

Chapter 26

1967-1968 NHL Gold Base

Timeline: 1967-1968.

How to Tell: NHL teams on oval gold base. A "man" face that many have suggested looks like Gordie Howe.

Set Profile: The last NHL set. Included two of the expansion teams, the St. Louis Blues and Los Angeles Kings. Not sure why the other four teams were not included, but no doll from North Stars, Flyers, Seals or Penguins has ever turned up.

Typical Flaws: The head mold is particularly thin and subject to paint peels and flakes. A flawless doll in this set is difficult to find. Paint chipping on the gold base also a concern.

Significant Variations: The Blues doll comes with two different uniform colors. Would say 70% come with a blue scheme and 30% with a gold. Although gold seems rarer, there is no premium, as of yet.

NHL gold base (Gordie Howe face) dolls. (author)

Historical Notes: First and last doll of Kings and Blues...Most of these dolls are scarce. I don't think they sold for very long or very well.

Stumbling Block: Looks like a three-way tie between the Leafs, Rangers and Bruins.

Want an example? The Gordie Howe face looks like it was popular in Gordie's old stomping grounds, Detroit. Still scarce, but more available than the others.

1967 Los Angeles Kings gold base or "Gordie Howe" face doll. (Jack McGuire)

1967-1968 NHL Gold Base (Gordie Howe)

Team	RI	EX	NM	M
Boston Bruins	9/9	$300	$450	$600
Chicago Blackhawks	5/6	$125	$175	$250
Detroit Redwings	4/6	$100	$175	$250
Los Angeles Kings	8/8	$225	$350	$500
Montreal Canadiens	8/8	$200	$350	$450
New York Rangers	9/9	$300	$400	$600
St. Louis Blues (gold and blue jerseys)	8/8	$275	$375	$500
Toronto Maple Leafs	9/9	$300	$450	$550

1967 Boston Bruins gold base or "Gordie Howe" face doll. (Jack McGuire)

Chapter 27

Minor League Hockey & Oddballs

Timeline: 1962-1972.

How to Tell: Hockey players with boy faces in most cases. Mascot heads on San Diego Gulls and Baltimore Clippers.

Profile: Here you have a mixed bag of seemingly independent efforts. Hershey and Los Angeles Blades share same molds similar to 1962 NHL. Crusaders, Bruins (blue base!!!), Boston Braves, New England Whalers and Tres Krone all look like later models. None of these teams mentioned above have decals on the base. The Gulls and Eagles share the same base style as 1967 NHL gold, but with unique heads. The Buckaroos is all by himself. Johnstown and Port Huron are explained in guide. Late in the game, a hybrid porcelain/*papier mâché* 12-inch Rangers bank was produced. I have a reliable source who swears there is an Islander in the same style as well, but I have never seen it.

Typical Flaws: Like the 1967 NHL gold the San Diego Gulls suffers from paint flakes and peels. The Bears and Blades are prone to fading and base chipping.

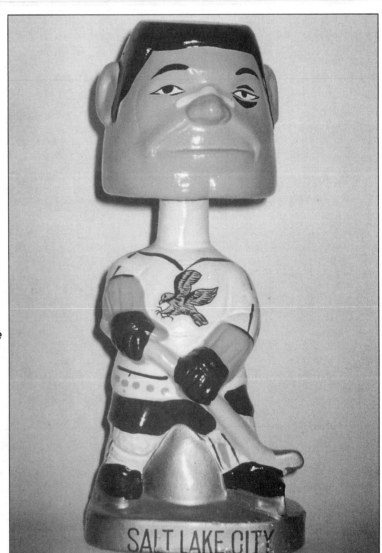

One of rarest hockey dolls. SLC Eagles. Note band aid on nose. (Bruce Stjernstrom)

Significant Variations: Not relevant here.

Historical Notes: Clippers doll unique in that the decals continue on the side of the base...SLC Eagles (very tough looking man face) doll adorned with a Band-Aid over nose...Ill-fated WHA with two representatives, the Cleveland Crusaders and New England Whalers...Only example (Blades) of a Los Angeles minor league team...Only examples of a Major (Bruins) and Minor (Braves) League team sharing shelf space at the same time...Only example of a San Diego minor league team...Only example of a Baltimore minor league team.

Stumbling Block: Most all of these dolls quite rare. Salt Lake City and Portland would seem to be the rarest.

Want an example? Due to a small find a few years back, the Baltimore Clippers has been available up to now. It also comes in an illustrated box.

The Cleveland Crusaders were one of two WHA teams to have dolls. (Jack McGuire)

Minor League Hockey & Oddballs

Team	Base Color	EX	NM	M
Baltimore Clippers (Captain head)	Blue	$120	$170	$240
Boston Braves	Blue	$200	$300	$450
Boston Bruins	Blue	$100	$150	$200
Cleveland Crusaders (WHA franchise)	blue	$90	$130	$170
Hershey Bears	Blue	$200	$300	$400
* Johnstown Jets	Blue	$200	$275	$350

The San Diego Gulls is a great mascot doll. It's almost impossible in mint. (Jack McGuire)

Team	Base Color	EX	NM	M
Los Angeles Blades	Light blue	$150	$220	$330
NE Whalers (WHA franchise)	Blue	$300	$450	$600
New York Rangers 12-inch bank	-	$100	$180	$240

This oddball Boston Bruins doll will cost about 25% of a 1962 Bruins doll. (Jack McGuire)

Team	Base Color	EX	NM	M
* Port Huron Flags	Red	$250	$350	$450
Port Buckaroos	Blue	$300	$425	$550
SLC Eagles	Gold	$500	$900	$1700
SD Gulls (bird head)	Gold	$225	$350	$450
Tres Krone (Swedish team)	Blue	$200	$300	$400

These two dolls were originally Red Wings (PH) and Leafs (JJ) dolls that were given a makeover to match the Minor League teams. They are considered "original" as work was done in the early-1960s.

Baltimore Clippers mascot doll. (author)

Chapter 28

Basketball Dolls & Lil Dribblers

BASKETBALL

Timeline: 1961-1971.

How to Tell: For regular basketball bobbing head doll, three (Knicks, Lakers and Globetrotters) are on a square base. The rest on round gold bases. Lil Dribblers are on an oval-shaped gold base.

Set Profile: Basketball was not on the minds of bobbing head distributors. Only three dolls from the early-1960s and a few more from the 1970s. The Lil

Dribblers although not a bobbing head (the ball is spring mounted to "bounce" from the hand), is close enough in characteristics and size to include. Again, the Lil Dribblers is a far from complete set, including teams only from East and Midwest.

Typical Flaws: Black players in gold base set usually victim of paint peeling. San Diego Rockets always a paint problem. Lil Dribblers are very sturdy, but sometimes missing the ball.

Significant Variations: None, although be sure when purchasing a Sonics (Japanese) doll that it has a yellow uniform. A Sonics with a white uniform came out

Sonics black player. (Bruce Stjernstrom)

in the 1970s (along with an equally worthless Blazers) and is extremely common.

Historical Notes: Late-1960s gold base set came with only three franchises on West Coast. Sonics and Lakers also had black player companion piece. San Diego Rockets seemingly did not...Only doll of San Diego Rockets (now in Houston)...Knicks Lil Dribblers and Knicks banks found *en masse* at Madison Square Garden in the early-1990s, and they're common as dirt now.

Stumbling Block: The two black dolls of the Sonics and Lakers are quite rare. In the Lil Dribblers set, the 76ers and Bullets white players are the toughest. The early (1962) Lakers and Knicks square bases also very difficult.

Want an example? No trouble with Knicks Lil Dribblers mentioned earlier. Lakers gold base also discovered in large quantities about eight years ago.

Basketball Dolls

Team	Base Color	EX	NM	M
Boston Celtics (no base decal)	Gold Round	$90	$150	$300
Generic Basketball Player	-	$12	$15	$25
Generic Kissing Pair	-	$15	$25	$35
Harlem Globetrotters (holding suitcase, 1962)	Blue or Green	$200	$325	$475

1962 Los Angeles Lakers green base. (Jack McGuire)

Team	Base Color	EX	NM	M
Los Angeles Lakers (1962)	Green Square	$175	$250	$425
Los Angeles Lakers (1967-68)	Gold Round	$35	$50	$60
Los Angeles Lakers (black player)	Gold Round	$150	$230	$300
New York Knicks (1962)	Orange Square	$180	$250	$450
New York Knicks 12-inch bank (black player)	-	$15	$25	$35
New York Knicks 12-inch bank (white player)	-	$15	$25	$35
San Diego Rockets (1967-68)	Gold Round	$150	$225	$275
Seattle Sonics (yellow jersey)	Gold Round	$125	$200	$325
Seattle Sonics (black player)	Gold Round	$175	$275	$350

Very colorful Globetrotter doll. Also comes in Lil Dribbler style. (Jack McGuire)

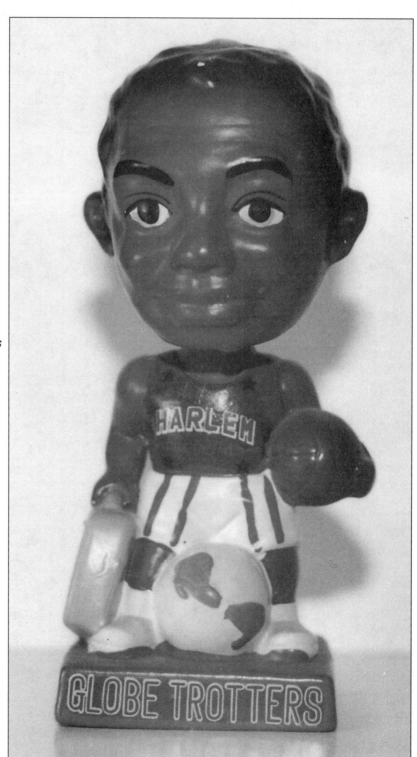

An original Sonics in yellow uniform—not to be con-fused with extremely common 1970s edition with white uniform. (Jack McGuire)

This Knicks doll is one of two dolls in square base bas-ketball "set." (Jack McGuire)

Lil Dribblers

Team	White Player	Black Player
Baltimore	$300-$330	$175-$200
Chicago Bulls	$130-$150	$100-$110
Detroit Pistons	$110-$130	$110-$130
Milwaukee Bucks	$70-$80	$60-$70
New York Knicks	$15-$25	$15-$25
Philadelphia 76ers	$225-$250	$150-$175
Globetrotter	-	$70-$90

76ers black player Lil Dribbler. (Jack McGuire)

Chicago Bulls white player Lil Dribbler. (Jack McGuire)

Chapter 29

Non-Sports Dolls

NON-SPORTS

We'll change format here, as there's no way to lump these together as a "set" or treat them alike.

Political Dolls: The creators showed a sense of humor with these dolls, as they had sayings on base such as these: Kruschev (Banging Shoe)—"There's no business like shoe business." Mao—"So who do you think brought Asian Flu." Kennedy (in football gear)—"I don't care if you are attorney general you were off sides." Eisenhower *does not* have his name on the base (some may put a sticker on base to add legitimacy and/or increase the likelihood of sale). The Big Four—JFK, Castro, Kruschev and Mao—all came in custom boxes. The Communist kissing pair was found in small quantity a few years back. The Camelot (JFK and Jackie) kissing pair always been extremely rare.

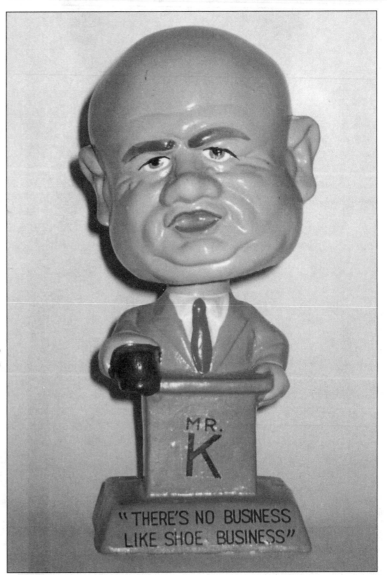

Kruschev: "There's no business like shoe business." (Bruce Stjernstrom)

Advertising Dolls: Rocky Taconites head has an actual covering of taconite…Colonel Sanders can have many different base decals…Always check the feet of Fall City doll. Most all are probably repaired there. Very weak area…Red Goose, Fall City and Mr. Peanut are "hip nodders" (bobs at hip instead of head)…Mr. Peanut should be carrying a cane, but it is almost always gone…Most advertising dolls were seemingly point-of-sale promotional items. Most of them are quite rare…Reddy Kilowatt is not the figure (electric man) most would expect. Instead it's a cowboy motif…Happy Homer would have to be the most detailed doll of all. Head is a house with corners, roof, windows, doors etc. Great example of bobbing head art…West-Tech Security was most likely last advertising doll made, judging by composition. Famous, as it turns out, from O.J. Simpson trial. "Subby" has "Groton" (CT) embossed on rear of base…Beware of fake Indy 500 dolls (generic cars and drivers with added decals)…Unisphere has "US Steel" stamp on bottom of base. Also come with custom box reading "Unisphere with bobbing action"…Tokyo Olympics most likely only sold in Japan. Five different events were represented by kissing pairs.

Cartoon Characters: Beetle Baily dolls were most likely the first made. Sculptured by "Kain." Probably least popular due to their very small heads…Peanuts dolls had *papier mâché* miniatures made in Korea in 1970s. Larger Peanuts undoubtedly made in large numbers, but most were played with and today are quite scarce in mint condition. Beethoven decal on Schroeder's chest is quite often chipped away…Warner Brothers dolls almost impossible to find in mint. A great deal of highlights and detail. Many of these dolls have been repaired, so look closely. Daffy Duck and Sylvester the Cat dolls are claimed to exist, but I have never seen them…Lil Abner dolls came out in 1975 and were made in Korea.

TV, Monsters, etc.: Large find of Dr. Kildare and Ben Casey (MIB) makes these rarer in VG than in gem mint. Vince Edwards (Ben Casey) facsimile autograph on rear of base is unique in doll world…Frankenstein, Wolfman and Phantom are incredibly rare. Have never seen one that wasn't damaged or repaired…Lad a Dog only bobbing head that has a movie tie-in…Real Bozo (very rare, beware of generic clowns offered as such) has "Capitol Records" stamp on bottom of base…Charlie Weaver comes with or without decal on base.

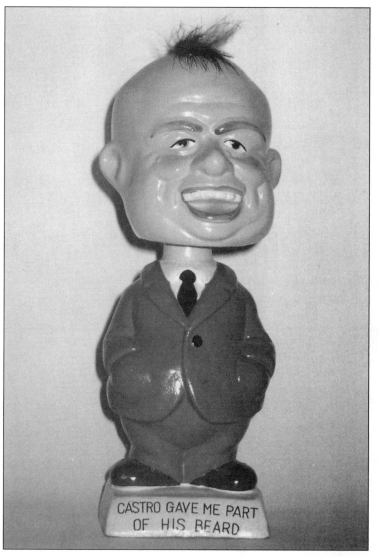

Kruschev: "Castro gave me part of his beard."
(Bruce Stjernstrom)

115

Celebrities, Musicians, etc.: Knock 20% off Beatles price without box...Plastic mini Beatles are most likely recent knockoffs...Repro regular size Beatles are known to exist. Best clue is Ringo's face. They did not get that right, otherwise it's hard to tell the difference...Donnie Osmond in see through panel custom box, also dated 1972...NASA astronaut only doll featuring a government agency.

Disney: Seems to be an even divide between "Disneyland" and "Disney World" dolls...Hang tags (extremely rare) on green based Disney dolls can increase value about 10%...Early Disney dolls in porcelain are one of the few pieces desired by *papier mâché* doll collectors...Last Disney World dolls made in Korea

Very rare Mao: "So who you think start Asian Flu?" (Bruce Stjernstrom)

Political Dolls

Doll	RI	EX	NM	M
Castro	6	$100	$150	$300
Castro/Kruschev (kissing pair)	6	$150	$250	$325
Democrat Donkey	2	$25	$40	$60
"Eisenhower"	6	$80	$140	$210

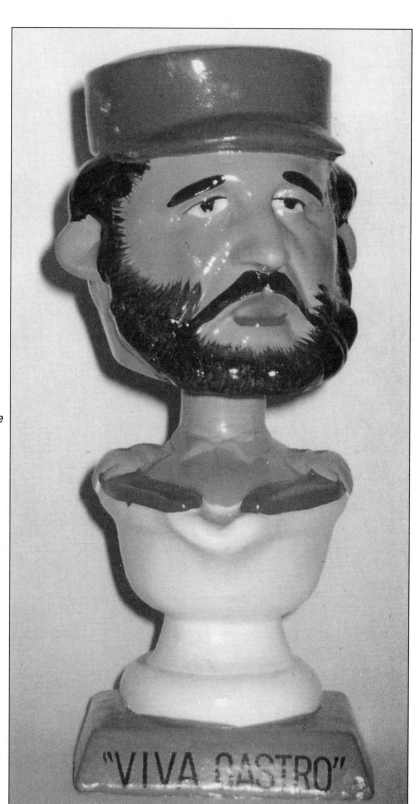

Castro: "Viva Castro." Many of these have turned up MIB. (Bruce Stjernstrom)

Doll	RI	EX	NM	M
John F. Kennedy (football player)	8	$250	$450	$700
John F. Kennedy, "Bronze"	10	$200	$350	$600
Jack/Jackie Kennedy (kissing pair)	10	$400	$800	$1,200
Kruschev, "Banging Shoe"	8	$225	$350	$500
Kruschev, "Castro's Beard"	9	$200	$300	$450
Mao	9	$250	$400	$700
"Nixon For President" (elephant)	7	$125	$200	$300
Republican Elephant (no mention about Nixon)	3	$30	$50	$65

The more common of two JFK dolls. "I don't care if you are attorney general you were off side!!" (Bruce Stjernstrom)

"Eisenhower" doll. Any decal on base is fake. (Bruce Stjernstrom)

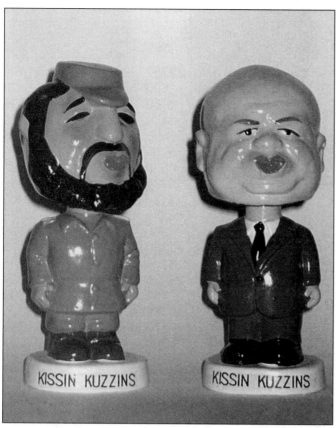

"Kissin' Kuzzins" Castro and Kruschev kissing pair. (Bruce Stjernstrom)

Very rare Jack and Jackie kissing pair. (Bruce Stjernstrom)

Political elephant and donkey. Another set has characters giving the "V" sign. They are the same value. (Jack McGuire)

Advertising

Doll	RI	EX	NM	M
Big Boy	8	$600	$750	$1,200
* Big Tex (Texas State Fair mascot)	8	$60	$90	$120
Bob Low Island	10	$175	$250	$400
Brylcreem (kissing pair)	7	$150	$250	$325
Campbell's Kids (pair)	10	$200	$300	$500
Colonel Sanders (*papier mâché*)	5	$100	$135	$180
Colonel Sanders (plastic)	3	$30	$50	$80
Fall City Beer (16-inch)	8	$150	$225	$325
Groton, Connecticut "Subby"	9	$100	$150	$400
Happy Homer	8	$150	$250	$375
Icey	8	$50	$60	$80
Indians with state or city stickers	5	$30	$50	$70
Indy 500 (car and driver)	9	$150	$300	$600
Indy 500 (standing driver)	8	$100	$175	$300
Inky Dinky (Ice Follies)	5	$40	$60	$80
Jockey (with racetrack sticker)	-	$60	$80	$100
Jockey (no racetrack sticker)	-	$50	$70	$90
KC Piston	6	$125	$200	$250
Knott's Berry Farm	10	$175	$250	$500

Indy 500 driver and car. Beware of fake decals. (Bruce Stjernstrom)

Doll	RI	EX	NM	M
L.A. County Fair Pig	8	$80	$130	$200
Little Profit (Chrysler dealers)	4	$40	$60	$80
Mr. Peanut	6	$100	$150	$250
Natural Gas Genie	10	$240	$350	$650
NBC Wavy TV	8	$125	$175	$275
New York World's Fair Unisphere	5	$60	$80	$100
New York World's Fair Kissing Pair	7	$70	$90	$140
New York World's Fair Boy and Girl	10	$80	$130	$150
Nugget Casino	6	$100	$150	$235

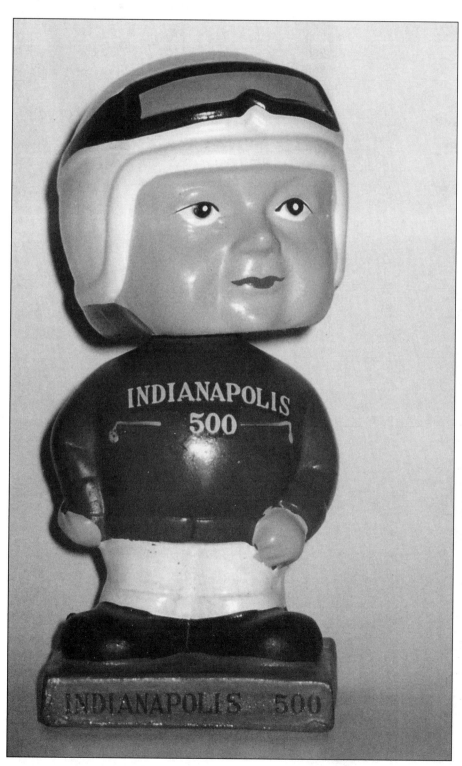

Indy 500 driver only. Tough doll to find in mint. (Bruce Stjernstrom)

Doll	RI	EX	NM	M
Oklahoma Indian Medicine Man	5	$50	$80	$110
Paul Revere Life (Toes-Up football player)	8	$80	$140	$200
Phillips 66	8	$200	$325	$450
Poll Parrot	10	$250	$500	$700
Ranier Brewing (*papier mâché*)	9	$150	$250	$350
Ranier Brewing (Styrofoam)	7	$40	$70	$120
Reddy Kilowatt	9	$300	$500	$750
Red Goose Shoes	6	$150	$240	$350
Rocky Taconite	10	$200	$350	$600
Six Flags (St. Louis) Boy or Girl	-	$140	$300	$500
Smokey the Bear, three versions, each	-	$150	$180	$230
Tokyo 1964 Olympics Kissing Pair	10	$200	$300	$400
Tom Pouce	10	$250	$400	$550
United Airlines	10	$300	$500	$700
Wally Waterlung	7	$125	$175	$240
Weatherbird Shoes	7	$175	$275	$350
West Tech Security	10	$125	$200	$350

* Has removable right arm.

Icey of Ice Capades. Rubber composition. (Bruce Stjernstrom)

Rocky Taconite. This very rare doll has actual taconite finish. (Bruce Stjernstrom)

One of three different Smokey the Bears. "Prevent Forest Fires" on base. (Bruce Stjernstrom)

"Last Chance Pete" from Nugget Casino in Sparks, Nevada. (Bruce Stjernstrom)

Extremely rare Natural Gas Genie that seems to have been of Canadian issue. (Bruce Stjernstrom)

Very rare and perhaps later Knott's Berry Farm. (Bruce Stjernstrom)

Big Tex from Texas State Fair. Note the removable/adjustable arm. (Bruce Stjernstrom)

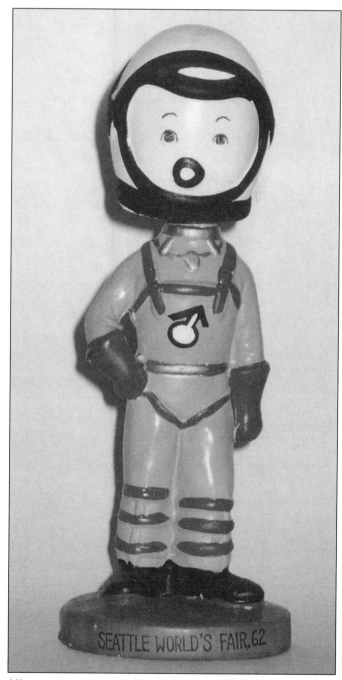

Ultra rare spaceman from Seattle World's Fair. (Bruce Stjernstrom)

KC Piston: "Let Casey go to bat for you." (Bruce Stjernstrom)

Mr. Peanut hip nodder. Note missing cane. It's hard to find one with a cane. (Bruce Stjernstrom)

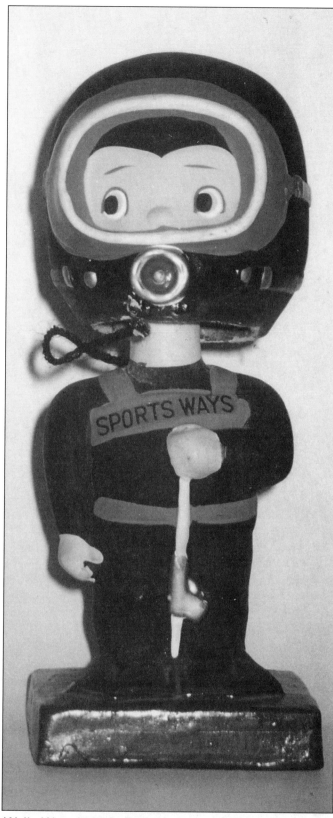

Wally Waterlung from Sportsways Scuba Gear. A poor choice of colors renders the decal on the base almost invisible. (Bruce Stjernstrom)

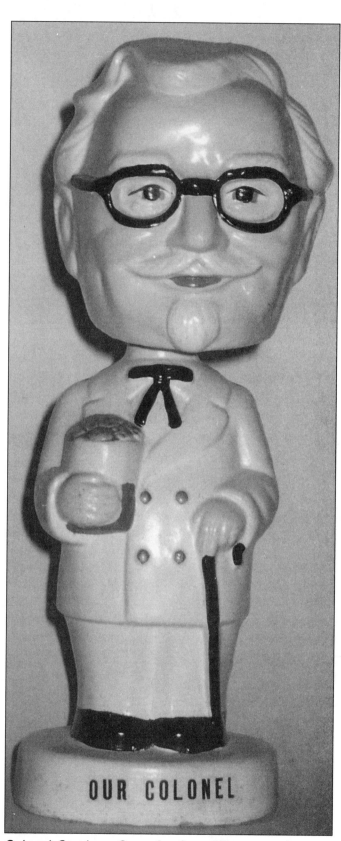

Colonel Sanders. One of a few different sayings on base. (Bruce Stjernstrom)

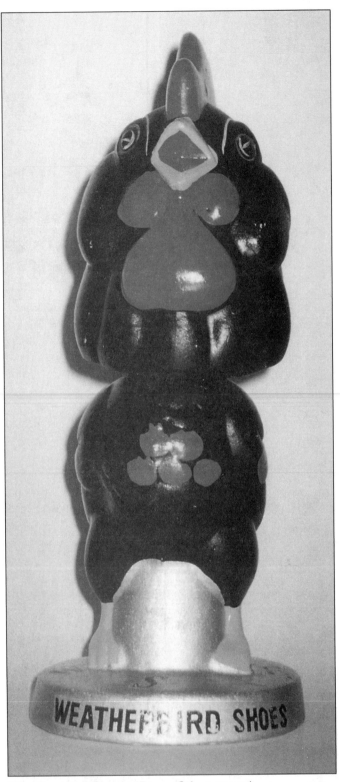

Weatherbird Shoes. (Bruce Stjernstrom)

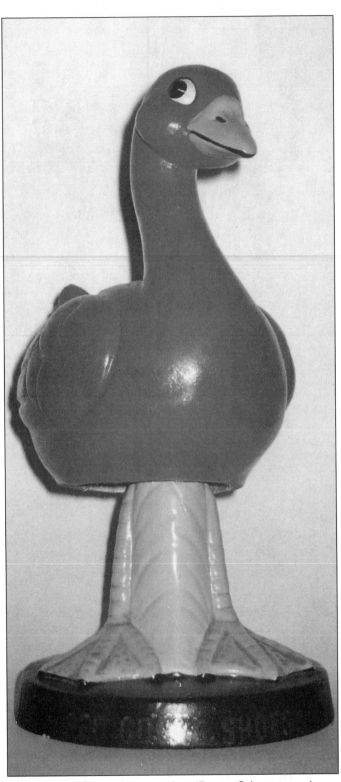

Red Goose Shoes hip nodder. (Bruce Stjernstrom)

Big Boy. One of most popular non-sports dolls. (Bruce Stjernstrom)

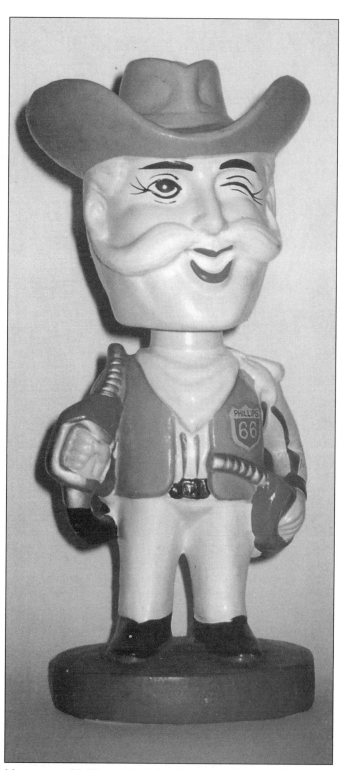

Very rare Phillips 66 doll. Beware of reproductions. There is no original black figure. (Bruce Stjernstrom)

The very elaborate Happy Homer. One of the author's favorites. (Bruce Stjernstrom)

NBC Wavy TV doll. (author)

Cartoon Characters

Doll	RI	EX	NM	M
Batman				
Batman	10	$500	$900	$1,800
Robin	10	$500	$800	$1,500
Beetle Baily				
Beetle Baily	4	$75	$100	$130
Lt. Fuzz	5	$90	$140	$170
Sgt. Snorkel	4	$70	$90	$125
Zero	5	$80	$120	$160
Peanuts				
Charlie Brown	5	$70	$90	$150
Charlie Brown (1970s miniature)	-	$35	$50	$70
Linus	5	$70	$90	$140
Lucy	5	$70	$90	$150
Lucy (1970s miniature)	-	$30	$45	$60
Pig Pen	7	$100	$150	$225
Schroeder	6	$70	$100	$160
Snoopy	4	$60	$90	$130
Snoopy (1970s mini, 3 different), each	-	$25	$40	$55
Woodstock (1970s mini)	-	$40	$60	$80

Linus from Peanuts cartoon. (Bruce Stjernstrom)

131

Doll	RI	EX	NM	M
Warner Brothers				
Bugs Bunny	8	$150	$300	$450
Elmer Fudd	8	$175	$250	$340
Foghorn Leghorn	8	$150	$250	$450
Porky Pig	9	$150	$350	$450
Speedy Gonzales	9	$200	$350	$550
Tweety	8	$175	$240	$340
Wile E. Coyote	7	$150	$225	$290
Yosemite Sam	8	$150	$250	$350
Others				
Alvin (Dennis the Menace knock-off)	7	$80	$120	$160
Dick Tracy	10	$350	$900	$2,000
Lil Abner Characters, 1975, each	-	$60	$80	$100
Popeye	9	$300	$500	$800

One of the rarest Warner Bros. dolls—Speedy Gonzales. (Bruce Stjernstrom)

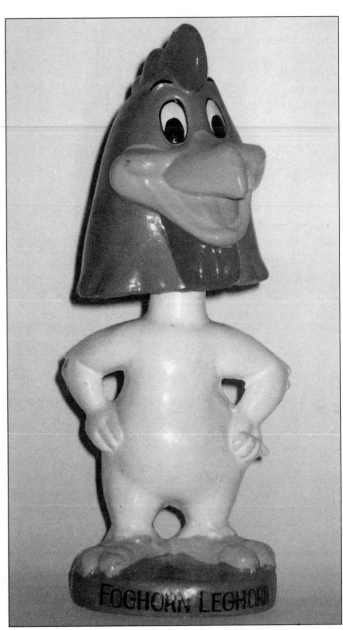

Foghorn Leghorn from WB set. (Bruce Stjernstrom)

Bugs Bunny from WB set. (Bruce Stjernstrom)

Tweety Bird from WB set. (Bruce Stjernstrom)

Wile E. Coyote from WB set. (Bruce Stjernstrom)

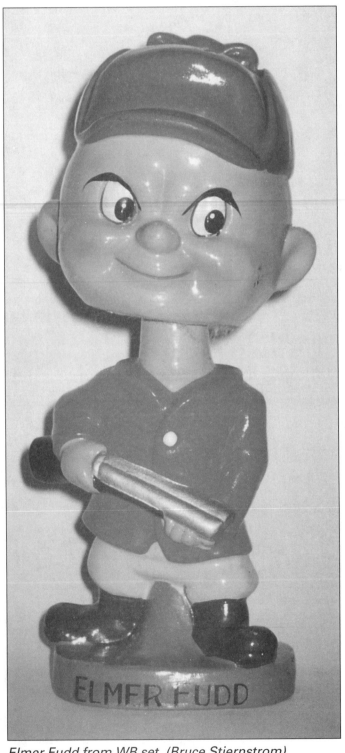

Elmer Fudd from WB set. (Bruce Stjernstrom)

WB's Porky Pig. (Bruce Stjernstrom)

1970s Lil Abner dolls. (Bruce Stjernstrom)

Incredibly rare Batman (two are known). (Bruce Stjernstrom)

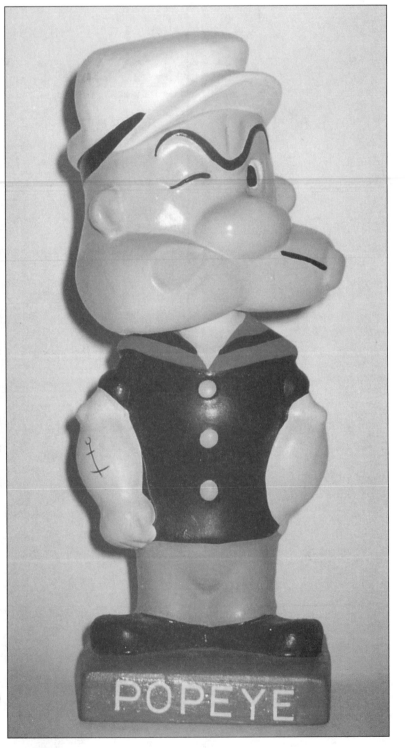

Less than five are known. (Bruce Stjernstrom)

Probably less than five in existence. (Bruce Stjernstrom)

Lt. Fuzz doll from Beetle Baily. (author)

TV/Movie Characters, Studios and Monsters

Doll	RI	EX	NM	M
Ben Casey	4	$60	$90	$130
Bozo	10	$300	$450	$800
Charlie Weaver	6	$80	$140	$200
Danny Kaye (kissing pair)	8	$140	$220	$350
Dobie Gillis	8	$140	$240	$325
Dr. Kildare	4	$60	$90	$130
Frankenstein	10	$400	$750	$1,200
Lad A Dog	8	$135	$175	$240
Maynard Krebs	8	$150	$230	$325
Oodles the Duck	10	$200	$300	$400
Phantom	10	$500	$850	$1,200
Roy Rogers	6	$100	$150	$225
Universal Studios (UST) Director	6	$80	$120	$170
UST Phantom of The Opera	9	$150	$350	$600
UST Keystone Kop	5	$60	$80	$120
Werewolf	10	$350	$600	$1200

Bozo's sidekick Oodles the duck, as rare as Bozo.
(Bruce Stjernstrom)

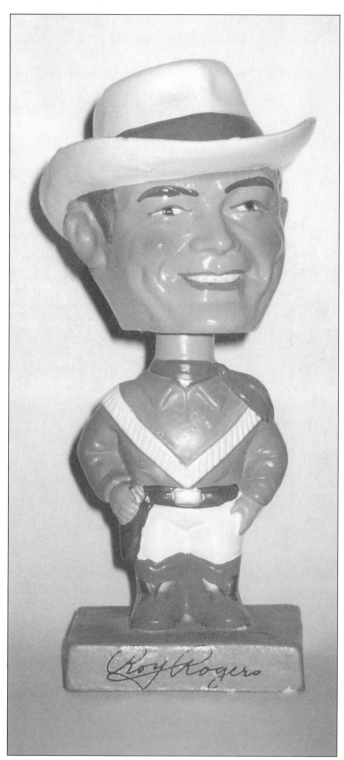

Roy Rogers. (Bruce Stjernstrom)

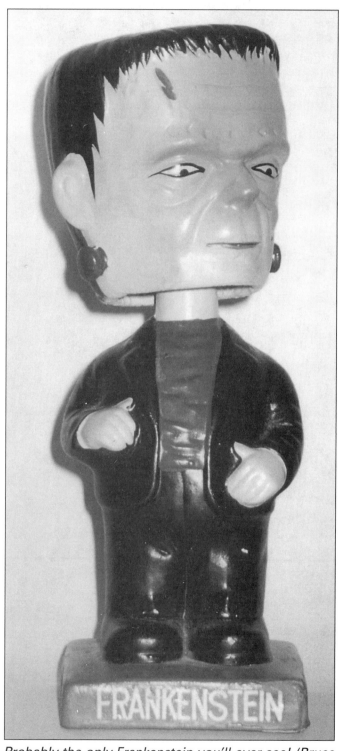

Probably the only Frankenstein you'll ever see! (Bruce Stjernstrom)

Rare Wolfman. (Bruce Stjernstrom)

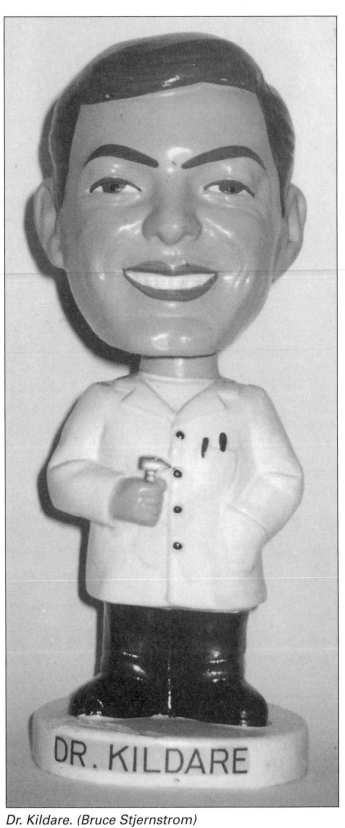

Dr. Kildare. (Bruce Stjernstrom)

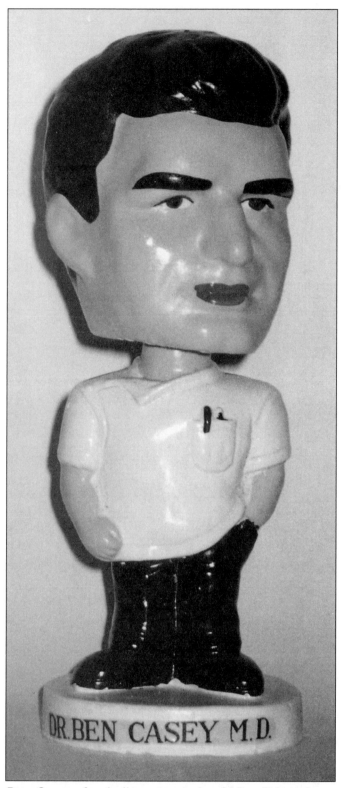

Ben Casey, facsimile autograph of Vice Edwards on rear of base. (Bruce Stjernstrom)

Charlie Weaver; comes with or without base decal. (Bruce Stjernstrom)

Kissing pair, Danny Kaye and friend. (Bruce Stjernstrom)

Only movie doll: Lad a Dog. (Bruce Stjernstrom)

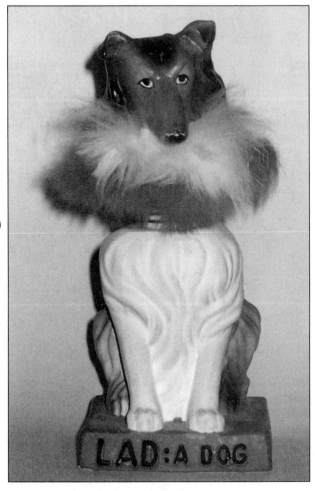

Celebrities, Musicians, Heroes, etc.

Doll	RI	EX	NM	M
Beatles (16-inch promos), for set	10	$4,000	$8,000	$12,000
Beatles (regular size), *with box*, for set	5	$350	$750	$1,300
Beatles (plastic mini)	1	$10	$15	$25
Davy Crockett	7	$75	$130	$180

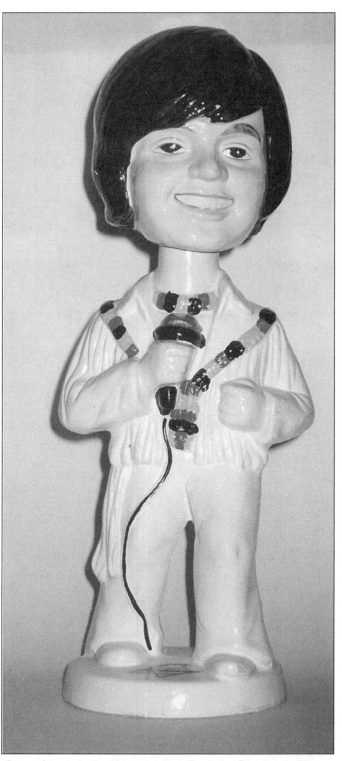

One of last dolls from Japan, Donnie Osmond. (Bruce Stjernstrom)

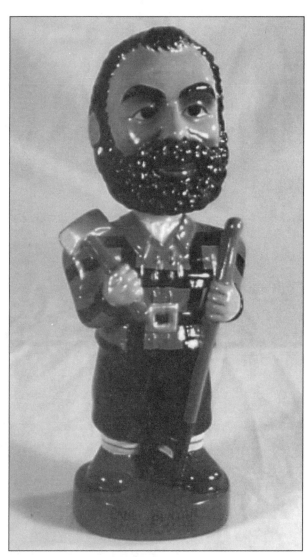

Paul Bunyan, Bangor, Maine. (author)

Doll	RI	EX	NM	M
NASA Astronaut	10	$100	$200	$350
Paul Bunyan, "Trees of Mystery"	7	$50	$75	$125
Paul Bunyan, "Little People at Feet"	7	$75	$125	$175
Donnie Osmond	7	$80	$120	$170
Santa Claus (many different)	4	$50	$80	$75-$200
Topo Gigio (many different)	3	$40	$60	$80

Santa sports dolls. (author)

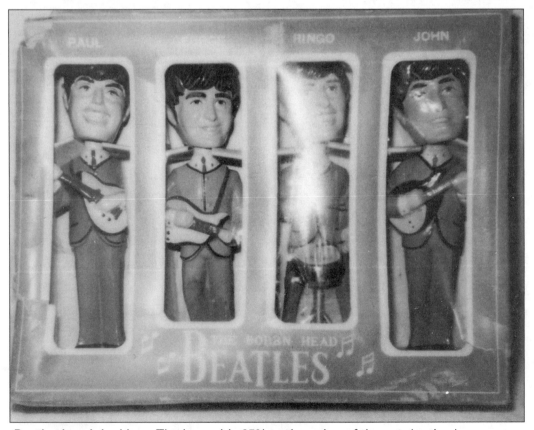

Beatles in original box. The box adds 25% to the value of the set. (author)

Disneyland/Disney World Series

Doll	RI	EX	NM	M
Donald Duck (early porcelain)	9	$60	$100	$175
Donald Duck (early DL, big head)	9	$70	$140	$200
Donald Duck (DL)	4	$50	$80	$120
Goofy DL	3	$60	$80	$110
Goofy DW	3	$50	$70	$90
Mickey Mouse (DL, big head)	9	$90	$150	$240
Mickey Mouse (DL)	5	$70	$90	$120
Mickey Mouse (DW)	6	$60	$80	$110

These dolls have either "Disneyland" (DL) or "Disney World" (DW) on base.

Disney's Pluto on green base with original hang tag.
(Bruce Stjernstrom)

Donald Duck Disneyland and Disney World dolls.
(author)

Disney, Round Green Base

Doll	RI	EX	NM	M
Donald Duck	4	$50	$70	$90
Mickey Mouse	4	$50	$70	$90
Pluto	3	$60	$80	$100
Winnie the Pooh	8	$120	$200	$350

Perhaps 10% premium for hang tags on green bases.

Disney, Other

Doll	RI	EX	NM	M
Goofy, Donald, Mickey in car	9	$100	$150	$250
Florida Orange Bird (1970s plastic)	7	$30	$40	$50

Kissing Pairs (base decal all important)

For those listed below, the "Happy Kids" location (Scotland, Russia, etc.) is on base of one doll, and "Happy Kids" is on the other. All are in native dress.

The following list is what is now known. I'm sure there are others. This is a colorful and interesting set and are all 8-10 in rarity. Price is per set.

Location	EX	NM	M
Alaska	$80	$100	$150
Hawaii	$100	$150	$250
India	$60	$90	$120
Japan	$50	$70	$90
Mexico	$50	$70	$90
Russia	$60	$90	$120
Scotland	$60	$80	$100
Spain	$60	$80	$100
USA	$50	$70	$90

With no decal or "Let's Kiss" on base, similar dolls are worth $20-$40 per set.

Rumpus Room dolls. (author)

Rumpus Room dolls. (author)

Minor Sports (bowling, golf, tennis, etc.)

Doll	RI	EX	NM	M
Surfing Boy and Girl	10	$100	$150	$200
Wedding Pair, for set	3	$25	$40	$60
The Twisters	-	$60	$80	$100
Florida or California Orange and Lemon, each	-	$40	$55	$70

Rumpus Room

There are at least 14 different "Weirdo" or "gag" dolls available. They can be identified by their wood base with a stamp on bottom reading: "A Rumpus Room Original, 1961 St. Pierre & Patterson." Dolls range in price from $60-$140 each.

Catch-Alls

Some of the more popular and valuable non-sports dolls not included in above categories.

Doll	EX	NM	M
Aloha Girls (lots of repros), originals	$20	$30	$40
Cleopatra	$40	$50	$60
Beatnik Bowler, Golfer, Fisherman, each	$70	$85	$100
Confederate Soldier	$40	$50	$60
Weirdo Boxer	$100	$120	$160
Space Boy/Girl with pin cushion rear, each	$50	$60	$70
"Mod" car (with different #s) driver. Two different sizes, several colors $100-$130			
Old King Cole	$70	$120	$160

Nearly Worthless Dolls ($10-$25)

- Kissing pair, Oriental
- Oriental singles
- Generic animals
- Generic bums, clowns, lovable losers, etc., etc.

These "Loser" dolls are of almost no value. (author)

Chapter 30

Post-Japan (1972-Present)

POST-JAPAN

In my mind, when the dolls stopped being produced in Japan (to a very small extent Korea) and in *papier mâché*, they lost everything. Attempts have been made over the years to produce the dolls in different materials and countries, but no effort has ever recaptured the original "magic." I find the charm of today's dolls to be extremely forced. I will leave the readers to make their own judgments on the various attributes of these post-Japan dolls. I can tell you that few are collected seriously and fewer still are worth more than the initial retail price. Collect them if you like, but my commentary ends here.

1970s Plastic

Baseball Dolls in box ($20-$40); no box $15-$30 (made in Taiwan)

Football Dolls with no belly showing, in box ($15-$25); no box ($10-$15)

Football Dolls with belly showing, in box ($15-$25); no box 10-$15)

Football Dolls "Running Back" ($15-$30)

Football Doll "OU" ($10-$15)

Later day plastic. Garage sale prices too high for these. (Jack McGuire)

1970s plastic football "running back" left and right. In the center is a 1960s prototype from which they probably were inspired. Note the two different plastic styles. (Jack McGuire)

1970s plastic baseball. (Jack McGuire)

1970s plastic Henry Aaron doll. The custom box is almost always included. (author)

1970s plastic. A few teams were made in this style. All are rare, but they are not valuable. (Jack McGuire)

1970s plastic football "no belly" and "belly." (Jack McGuire)

1970s Ceramic

Doll	EX	NM	M
Indians, yellow uniform	$60	$80	$100
Indians, white uniform	$50	$70	$90
Pirates, yellow uniform	$50	$70	$90
Yankees, green base	$40	$60	$80
Seattle Sonics, white uniform	$15	$20	$25
Portland Blazers	$15	$20	$25

1970s yellow uniform Pirates. (Jack McGuire)

Indians with yellow uniform. Indians never had such a color! (Jack McGuire)

1980s dolls

Doll	Price
Golden Era Babe Ruth	$25
Golden Era Lou Gehrig	$25
Golden Era Joe Jackson	$25
Golden Era Ty Cobb	$25
Golden Era Honus Wagner	$60
Golden Era Bronko Nagurski	$50
Imus	$200

"Golden Era" Ruth. (Jack McGuire)

"Golden Era" Gehrig. (Jack McGuire)

Twins Enterprises (1980s)

All with green bases. The bottom of base will have a piece of felt or nothing but a circular hole

Doll	**Price Range**
First issue, all teams with bat, each	$25-$40
First issue, all teams with ball, each	$40-$60
Second issue, more pronounced bellies, each	$10-$15

Comparison of Twins Enterprises dolls: 1982 dolls on the right and left; 1985-1988 doll in the center. The ball example is quite scarce. (Jack McGuire)

St. Louis Cardinals Twins Enterprises doll from 1985-1988. (author)

1990s Dolls (not including dolls for sale at moment)

Doll	Price Range
Negro League players	$20-$30
Sam's Dolls (not including 3-doll sets that may cost more)	$10-$70
Warner Brothers, each	$20-$35
Pete's Wicked Ale	$25-$35
Fossil Watch	$15-$25
Hayden Fry and Herkie Hawk	$20-$30
"Catcher Style," Twins Enterprises	$15-$25

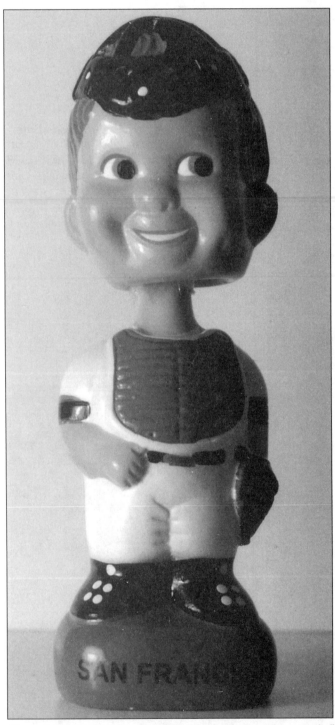

One for the future. A very limited "catcher style" 1990s issue. (Jack McGuire)

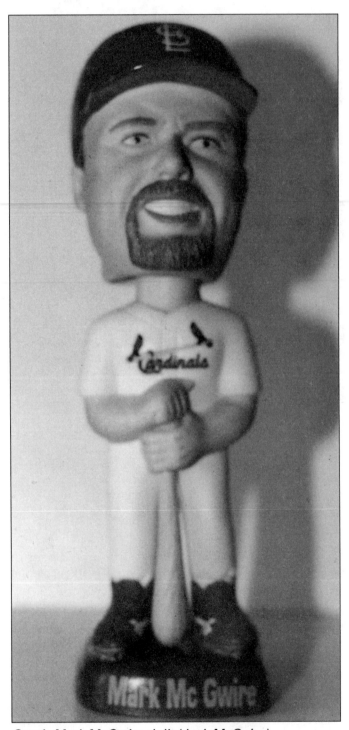

Sam's Mark McGwire doll. (Jack McGuire)

New Sylvester from Warner Brothers. (Jack McGuire)

New Tweety from Warner Brothers. (Jack McGuire)

Baseball Bobbing Head Team Checklist

(Japan-Made Dolls)

Anaheim Angels
1961-1962 White Base Miniatures
1961-1963 White Base
1963-1965 Green Base

Atlanta Braves
1966-1971 Gold Base

Baltimore Orioles
1960-1961 Square Color Base (diamond shape)
1961-1962 White Base Miniatures
1961-1963 White Base
1963-1965 Black Players
1963-1965 Green Base
1966-1971 Gold Base

Boston Red Sox
1960-1961 Square Color Base
1961-1962 White Base Miniatures
1961-1963 White Base
1963-1965 Black Players
1963-1965 Green Base (blue hat)
1963-1965 Green Base (red hat)
1966-1971 Gold Base
1970-72 Wedge Base

California Angels
1966-1971 Gold Base
1970-72 Wedge Base

Chicago Cubs
1960-1961 Square Color Base
1961-1962 White Base Miniatures
1961-1963 White Base
1963-1965 Black Players
1963-1965 Green Base
1966-1971 Gold Base
1970-72 Wedge Base

Chicago White Sox
1961-1962 White Base Miniatures
1961-1963 White Base
1963-1965 Black Players
1963-1965 Green Base
1966-1971 Gold Base

Cincinnati Reds
1960-1961 Square Color Base
1961-1962 White Base Miniatures
1961-1963 White Base
1963-1965 Black Players
1963-1965 Green Base
1966-1971 Gold Base

Cleveland Indians
1961-1962 White Base Miniatures
1961-1963 White Base
1963-1965 Black Players
1963-1965 Green Base
1966-1971 Gold Base

Detroit Tigers
1961-1962 White Base Miniatures
1961-1963 White Base
1963-1965 Black Players
1963-1965 Green Base
1966-1971 Gold Base

Houston Colt .45s
1961-1962 White Base Miniatures
1961-1963 White Base
1963-1965 Black Players
1963-1965 Green Base

Houston Astros
1961-1962 White Base Miniatures
1961-1963 White Base
1966-1971 Gold Base (shooting star decal)
1966-1971 Gold Base (regular decal)
1970-72 Wedge Base (blue hat)
1970-72 Wedge Base (orange hat)

Kansas City A's
1961-1963 White Base
1963-1965 Green Base (light blue hat)
1963-1965 Green Base (dark blue hat)
1966-1971 Gold Base

Kansas City Royals
1966-1971 Gold Base
1970-72 Wedge Base

Los Angeles Angels
1960-1961 Square Color Base
1961-1962 White Base Miniatures
1961-1963 White Base
1963-1965 Black Players
1963-1965 Green Base

Los Angeles Dodgers
1961-1962 White Base Miniatures
1961-1963 White Base
1963-1965 Black Players
1963-1965 Green Base
1966-1971 Gold Base

Milwaukee Braves
1961-1962 White Base Miniatures
1961-1963 White Base
1963-1965 Black Players
1963-1965 Green Base

Milwaukee Brewers
1966-1971 Gold Base

Minnesota Twins
1960-1961 Square Color Base
1961-1962 White Base Miniatures
1963-1965 Green Base
1966-1971 Gold Base
1970-72 Wedge Base

Montreal Expos
1966-1971 Gold Base

New York Mets
1960-1961 Square Color Base
1961-1962 White Base Miniatures
1961-1963 White Base
1963-1965 Black Players
1963-1965 Green Base
1966-1971 Gold Base

New York Yankees
1960-1961 Square Color Base
1961-1962 White Base Miniatures
1961-1962 White Base Miniatures (Mantle)
1961-1962 White Base Miniatures (Maris)
1961-1963 White Base
1961-1963 White Base (Mantle)
1961-1963 White Base (Maris)
1963-1965 Black Players
1963-1965 Green Base
1966-1971 Gold Base

Oakland A's
1966-1971 Gold Base (white uniform)
1966-1971 Gold Base (yellow uniform)

Philadelphia Phillies
1961-1962 White Base Miniatures
1961-1963 White Base
1963-1965 Black Players
1963-1965 Green Base
1966-1971 Gold Base

Pittsburgh Pirates
1960-1961 Square Color Base
1961-1962 White Base Miniatures
1961-1963 White Base
1961-1963 White Base (Clemente)
1963-1965 Green Base
1966-1971 Gold Base

St. Louis Cardinals
1961-1962 White Base Miniatures
1961-1963 White Base
1963-1965 Black Players
1963-1965 Green Base
1966-1971 Gold Base
1970-72 Wedge Base

San Diego Padres
1966-1971 Gold Base

San Francisco Giants
1960-1961 Square Color Base
1961-1962 White Base Miniatures
1961-1963 White Base
1961-1963 White Base (Mays, dark face)
1961-1963 White Base (Mays, light face)
1963-1965 Green Base
1966-1971 Gold Base
1966-1971 Gold Base (Mays)
1970-72 Wedge Base

Seattle Pilots
1966-1971 Gold Base

Texas Rangers
1966-1971 Gold Base

Washington Senators
1960-1961 Square Color Base
1961-1962 White Base Miniatures
1961-1963 White Base
1963-1965 Black Players
1963-1965 Green Base
1966-1971 Gold Base

Football Bobbing Head Team Checklist

(Japan-Made Dolls)

Atlanta Falcons
1961-1966 NFL "Toes-Up" Type
1965-1967 NFL Gold Base
1965-1967 NFL Gold Round Base/Realistic Face
1968-1970 NFL/AFL Round Gold Base "Merger Series"

Baltimore Colts
1960-1961 NFL Square Wood Base
1961-1963 NFL Square Regular Base
1960-1961 NFL 15-inch Promo Dolls
1962-1964 NFL Kissing Pairs
1961-1966 NFL "Toes-Up" Type
1962-1964 Black Players Toes-Up
1962-1964 NFL Kissing Pairs
1963-1964 NFL Square Gold Base (black and white players)
1965-1967 NFL Gold Base
1965-1967 NFL Gold Round Base/Realistic Face
1968-1970 NFL/AFL Round Gold Base "Merger Series"

Boston Patriots
1961-1962 AFL Round Base/Toes-Up
1962-1964 NFL Kissing Pairs
1965-1966 AFL Gold Base/Ear Pads
1968 Gold Base AFL
1968-1970 NFL/AFL Round Gold Base "Merger Series"

Buffalo Bills
1961-1962 AFL Round Base/Toes-Up
1962-1964 NFL Kissing Pairs
1965-1966 AFL Gold Base/Ear Pads
1968 Gold Base AFL
1968-1970 NFL/AFL Round Gold Base "Merger Series"

Chicago Bears
1960-1961 NFL Square Wood Base
1961-1963 NFL Square Regular Base
1960-1961 NFL 15-inch Promo Dolls
1962-1964 NFL Kissing Pairs
1961-1966 NFL "Toes-Up" Type
1962-1964 Black Players Toes-Up
1963-1964 NFL Square Gold Base
1965-1967 NFL Gold Base
1965-1967 NFL Gold Round Base/Realistic Face
1968-1970 NFL/AFL Round Gold Base "Merger Series"

Cincinnati Bengals
1968-1970 NFL/AFL Round Gold Base "Merger Series"

Cleveland Browns
1960-1961 NFL Square Wood Base
1961-1963 NFL Square Regular Base
1960-1961 NFL 15-inch Promo Dolls
1962-1964 NFL Kissing Pairs
1961-1966 NFL "Toes-Up" Type
1962-1964 Black Players Toes-Up
1965-1967 NFL Gold Base
1965-1967 NFL Gold Round Base/Realistic Face
1968 Gold Base AFL
1968-1970 NFL/AFL Round Gold Base "Merger Series"

Dallas Cowboys
1960-1961 NFL Square Wood Base
1961-1963 NFL Square Regular Base
1960-1961 NFL 15-inch Promo Dolls
1962-1964 NFL Kissing Pairs
1961-1966 NFL "Toes-Up" Type
1962-1964 Black Players Toes-Up
1965-1967 NFL Gold Base
1965-1967 NFL Gold Round Base/Realistic Face
1968-1970 NFL/AFL Round Gold Base "Merger Series"

Dallas Texans
1961-1962 AFL Round Base/Toes-Up

Denver Broncos
1961-1962 AFL Round Base/Toes-Up
1965 AFL Gold Base
1965-1966 AFL Gold Base/Ear Pads
1968 Gold Base AFL
1968-1970 NFL/AFL Round Gold Base "Merger Series"

Detroit Lions
1960-1961 NFL Square Wood Base
1961-1963 NFL Square Regular Base
1960-1961 NFL 15-inch Promo Dolls
1962-1964 NFL Kissing Pairs
1961-1966 NFL "Toes-Up" Type
1962-1964 Black Players Toes-Up
1963-1964 NFL Square Gold Base (black and white players)
1965-1967 NFL Gold Base

1965-1967 NFL Gold Round Base/Realistic Face
1968-1970 NFL/AFL Round Gold Base "Merger Series"

Green Bay Packers
1960-1961 NFL Square Wood Base
1961-1963 NFL Square Regular Base
1960-1961 NFL 15-inch Promo Dolls
1962-1964 NFL Kissing Pairs
1961-1966 NFL "Toes-Up" Type
1962-1964 Black Players Toes-Up
1965-1967 NFL Gold Base
1965-1967 NFL Gold Round Base/Realistic Face
1968-1970 NFL/AFL Round Gold Base "Merger Series"

Houston Oilers
1961-1962 AFL Round Base/Toes-Up
1965 AFL Gold Base
1965-1966 AFL Gold Base/Ear Pads
1968 Gold Base AFL (orange helmet)
1968-1970 NFL/AFL Round Gold Base "Merger Series"

Kansas City Chiefs
1965 AFL Toes-Up
1965-1966 AFL Gold Base/Ear Pads
1968 Gold Base AFL
1968-1970 NFL/AFL Round Gold Base "Merger Series"

Los Angeles Rams
1960-1961 NFL Square Wood Base
1961-1963 NFL Square Regular Base
1960-1961 NFL 15-inch Promo Dolls
1962-1964 NFL Kissing Pairs
1961-1966 NFL "Toes-Up" Type
1962-1964 Black Players Toes-Up
1968-1970 NFL/AFL Round Gold Base "Merger Series"

Miami Dolphins
1965 AFL Toes-Up
1965-1966 AFL Gold Base/Ear Pads
1968 Gold Base AFL
1968-1970 NFL/AFL Round Gold Base "Merger Series"

Minnesota Vikings
1961-1963 NFL Square Regular Base
1962-1964 NFL Kissing Pairs
1961-1966 NFL "Toes-Up" Type
1962-1964 Black Players Toes-Up
1963-1964 NFL Square Gold Base
1965-1967 NFL Gold Base

1965-1967 NFL Gold Round Base/Realistic Face
1968-1970 NFL/AFL Round Gold Base "Merger Series"

New England Patriots
1968-1970 NFL/AFL Round Gold Base "Merger Series"

New Orleans Saints
1965-1967 NFL Gold Base
1965-1967 NFL Gold Round Base/Realistic Face
1968-1970 NFL/AFL Round Gold Base "Merger Series"

New York Giants
1960-1961 NFL Square Wood Base
1961-1963 NFL Square Regular Base
1960-1961 NFL 15-inch Promo Dolls
1962-1964 NFL Kissing Pairs
1961-1966 NFL "Toes-Up" Type
1962-1964 Black Players Toes-Up
1963-1964 NFL Square Gold Base
1965-1967 NFL Gold Base
1968-1970 NFL/AFL Round Gold Base "Merger Series"

New York Jets
1965-1966 AFL Gold Base/Ear Pads
1968 Gold Base AFL
1968-1970 NFL/AFL Round Gold Base "Merger Series"

New York Titans
1961-1962 AFL Round Base/Toes-Up

Oakland Raiders
1961 Square Base
1961-1962 AFL Round Base/Toes-Up
1965-1966 AFL Gold Base/Ear Pads
1968 Gold Base AFL
1968-1970 NFL/AFL Round Gold Base "Merger Series"

Philadelphia Eagles
1960-1961 NFL Square Wood Base
1961-1963 NFL Square Regular Base
1960-1961 NFL 15-inch Promo Dolls
1962-1964 NFL Kissing Pairs
1961-1966 NFL "Toes-Up" Type
1962-1964 Black Players Toes-Up
1965-1967 NFL Gold Base
1965-1967 NFL Gold Round Base/Realistic Face
1968-1970 NFL/AFL Round Gold Base "Merger Series"

Pittsburgh Steelers

1960-1961 NFL Square Wood Base
1961-1963 NFL Square Regular Base
1960-1961 NFL 15-inch Promo Dolls
1962-1964 NFL Kissing Pairs
1961-1966 NFL "Toes-Up" Type
1962-1964 Black Players Toes-Up
1965-1967 NFL Gold Base
1968-1970 NFL/AFL Round Gold Base "Merger Series"

St. Louis Cardinals

1960-1961 NFL Square Wood Base
1961-1963 NFL Square Regular Base
1960-1961 NFL 15-inch Promo Dolls
1962-1964 NFL Kissing Pairs
1961-1966 NFL "Toes-Up" Type
1963-1964 NFL Square Gold Base (black and white players)
1965-1967 NFL Gold Round Base/Realistic Face
1968-1970 NFL/AFL Round Gold Base "Merger Series"

San Diego Chargers

1961-1962 AFL Round Base/Toes-Up
1965-1966 AFL Gold Base/Ear Pads
1968 Gold Base AFL

1968-1970 NFL/AFL Round Gold Base "Merger Series"

San Francisco 49ers

1960-1961 NFL Square Wood Base
1961-1963 NFL Square Regular Base
1960-1961 NFL 15-inch Promo Dolls
1962-1964 NFL Kissing Pairs
1961-1966 NFL "Toes-Up" Type
1962-1964 Black Players Toes-Up
1968-1970 NFL/AFL Round Gold Base "Merger Series"

Washington Redskins

1960-1961 NFL Square Wood Base
1961-1963 NFL Square Regular Base
1960-1961 NFL 15-inch Promo Dolls
1962-1964 NFL Kissing Pairs
1961-1966 NFL "Toes-Up" Type
1962-1964 Black Players Toes-Up
1963-1964 NFL Square Gold Base
1965-1966 AFL Gold Base/Ear Pads
1965-1967 NFL Gold Base
1965-1967 NFL Gold Round Base/Realistic Face
1968-1970 NFL/AFL Round Gold Base "Merger Series"

Hockey Bobbing Head Team Checklist

(Japan-Made Dolls)
Boston Bruins

1961-1963 NHL Square Base
1961-1963 NHL Miniature
1961-1963 Canadian "High Skates"
1962 Smaller "High Skates"
1967-1968 NHL Gold Base
1971 Blue Square Base

Chicago Blackhawks

1961-1963 NHL Square Base
1961-1963 NHL Miniature
1961-1963 Canadian "High Skates"
1962 Smaller "High Skates"
1967-1968 NHL Gold Base

Detroit Red Wings

1961-1963 NHL Square Base
1961-1963 NHL Miniature
1961-1963 Canadian "High Skates"
1962 Smaller "High Skates"
1967-1968 NHL Gold Base

Los Angeles Kings

1967-1968 NHL Gold Base

Montreal Canadiens

1961-1963 NHL Square Base
1961-1963 NHL Miniature
1961-1963 Canadian "High Skates"
1962 Smaller "High Skates"
1967-1968 NHL Gold Base

New York Rangers

1961-1963 NHL Square Base
1961-1963 NHL Miniature
1961-1963 Canadian "High Skates"
1962 Smaller "High Skates"
1967-1968 NHL Gold Base

St. Louis Blues

1967-1968 NHL Gold Base

Toronto Maple Leafs

1961-1963 NHL Square Base
1961-1963 NHL Miniature
1961-1963 Canadian "High Skates"
1962 Smaller "High Skates"
1967-1968 NHL Gold Base